MARRIAGE:

GOD'S LOVE AFFAIR VS. ARRANGEMENT

"The difference between God's intended marriage, a love affair, and an arrangement is in the 'why.' The motive reveals the 'why.'"

LOUIS L. FORTÉ
WITH DEBORAH L. RIVERA

Lovingforté LLC
Lancaster, CA

Marriage:
God's Love Affair vs. Arrangement

Copyright © 2010 - 2013 by Louis Forté and Deborah Rivera

Published by LOVINGFORTÉ LLC,
Lancaster, CA 93536

Cover illustration: Artist Ranilo Cabo
ranilocabo@yahoo.com

Library of Congress Control Number: 2013910321

ISBN 978-0-578-12312-7

This book is dedicated to my late wife, Sarita.

I also want to dedicate this book to the many beautiful couples who are destroying one another due to a lack of understanding.

It is my deepest desire that this book on marriage portrayed as a love affair will greatly influence pre-married and married couples all over the world to truly make their marriages love affairs. Yet, I want this book to benefit not only the couples but their children, their children's children, etc. Nothing is more beautiful than seeing couples love each other under the love covenant with their children watching them.

May the God of all creation, the Father of glory, keep you and bless you as you pursue this life of love in Jesus' name. Amen.

*"It is impossible to have life and be fulfilled without **your self**."*
Louis L. Forté

1

FOREWORD

"I applaud Mr. Forté on the thorough job he has done writing this book. I believe his book is an inspiration and guideline for many couples who will be joining in matrimony in the years to come. In a world that has left God's standard for marriage, a book like this will give us immediate biblical guidance toward making one of the greatest decisions in our life.

This book to me is tantamount to attending a pre-marriage school; it lays out and explains in detail what marriage is all about and the inherent responsibility of each spouse.

Mr. Forté's book is not just a book that gives us valuable knowledge on the subject of marriage, but it gives also much-needed wisdom from his own life on the subject of marriage.

I would personally recommend this book to anyone who is already married and anyone who is seriously contemplating marriage."

Pastor Tom Pickens
Senior Pastor of Antelope Valley Christian Center

INTRODUCTION

I enjoyed a beautiful relationship for 45 years with my late wife, Sarita, before losing her to a car accident in August 2009. Though we loved each other through all of the tests and trials of any marriage, it was during our first year that we truly lived a love affair—not by trying; we just did so naturally and beautifully. We truly loved each other and put no one above each other. As we were neither mature nor aware that what we were living was God's true purpose for marriage, we eventually made unwise decisions that forfeited putting each other first as we originally did. Our love affair changed into an arrangement.

Before Sarita's death, we were on our way back to that love affair we once shared in our beginning years.

Love is the most wonderful thing to which you can ever give yourself. This book was written to provide an understanding of this amazing reality and the true design for marriage. Understanding and living these principles will provide any couple excellent reasons to do what is needed to live a love affair.

"What air is to the body is what understanding is to the heart."
Deborah L. Rivera

ACKNOWLEDGMENTS

This book *could not have been written* without the loving guidance of the Holy Spirit.

For a period of about six months after the death of my wife in 2009, the Holy Spirit gave me words of wisdom and love for marriage along with the scriptures to reference what He gave me. I would hurry to write down what He said. Sometimes, He gave me these words of love when I was jogging, or driving, at work, or in the store. It really did not matter where I was; when He spoke, I would write it down. Over six months' time, I had many little pieces of paper with excerpts of His thoughts on marriage.

What is amazing about the Lord is that as the Holy Spirit just recently began to give me what I call now "God's intended design for marriage," *He long ago* began to prepare this book by placing these *same thoughts and ideas* for God's intended design for marriage in my daughter, Deborah Lavora Forté, now Deborah L. Rivera.

As I told Deborah what the Lord gave me, she disclosed that this was what the Lord had been developing in her through her childhood and with intensity in 1999. It was as if God were preparing a field and getting it ready to plant. Because of this same word God gave her, Deborah was able to put this book together in one month, writing it as if it were a river just constantly flowing. For her tremendous love and obedience to the Lord, I am *most* grateful.

When someone asks me, "Where did you get your information from? Where did you do your research?" I can only respond, "From the Holy Spirit and the Bible." ***All I did was obey when He spoke.*** Each new day, we see that from this field the Lord is preparing a harvest of His agape love to transform the lives of people around the world. This is His work…His plan. To Him be all the glory and thanks, for without Him, this book would never have been written.

Our deepest appreciation goes to Pastor Tom Pickens, our senior pastor and founder of Antelope Valley Christian Center, and First Lady Donna Pickens. We are deeply appreciative for their support of this book and all that they have done through the years. Again, our sincerest gratitude and thanks.

Also, a tremendous amount of gratitude goes to our cover designer, Ranilo Cabo, whose extraordinary gift of insight and skill was able to give us the image we were looking for in his first attempt; and our editor, Katherine Ungerecht, whose expertise is valued with many, many thanks. Thank you both for all the hard work you have done.

PREFACE

The title of this book, "Marriage: God's Love Affair vs. Arrangement," points ultimately to two very different lifestyles for a marriage between a man and a woman. The foundation for any marriage results from what these two people believe a marriage should be. From their beliefs, a marriage results. Everyone comes from many different cultures and backgrounds. Ideas people acquire during their lifetimes within their families, from society, from peers, etc. formulate their personal beliefs or philosophy on what marriage should be. This is very powerful, knowing that the end result of a man's life is from the choices this man chooses. Or, better said, his final decisions are influenced by his own personal belief system…his philosophy. The Bible says, "As a man thinketh in his heart, so is he" (Prov. 23:7). Therefore, what we choose to accept as truth, or what we choose as our belief system, is very powerful and consequential, knowing that whatever we choose will result in _our end_, whether life or death. Our loving and omnipotent God, our Father, put this powerful act within our ability, giving us the freedom to choose our own outcome. In His all-powerfulness, He does not control our choices. He sets forth His law in His Word…His design for life, and based on what we choose, His law will set forth our end result…life or death. This should make us take a second look at how we are arriving at the choices we make. What are we thinking concerning the marriage that _God_ (not man, not culture, not our past) created?

God said in Deuteronomy 30:19, "I have set before you life and death, blessing and cursing: therefore choose life…" We are to choose Him: in our marriages as well as in the rest of life.

Though the world's relative approach to marriage exists, it cannot substitute for God's original design for marriage and produce the same outcome for what He created marriage to be. So, to be clear, let's reference the world's relative approach to marriage as "an arrangement," which is based on many different ideas and philosophies but lacks God's original design. And because it lacks God's original design, it produces an outcome that lacks God's original purpose. Let's call God's original design for marriage "God's love affair." God's love affair will look like His original design...His love of oneness.

This book preferences marriage based on the law of first beginnings, which is the truest meaning or purest form of anything that God creates. God's *original design* is what He wants; sin altered God's original design, resulting in pain, suffering, and self-preservation (Gen. 2:24). God's design for marriage between one man and one woman, with Him as the source of life for this marriage, is the epitome of earthly living. ("Earthly living" meaning marriage, as it is the highest form of blessing and love within the human race or on earth. All things concerning human life on earth come from or surround the union between a man and a woman.) That is why God put the importance, blessing, and uniqueness of marriage on nothing else. God's design for marriage, God's love affair, is His plan for the earth to be inhabited (Gen. 2:28). God has not created or made anything in the *earth's realm, on humanity's level*, that can equal or compare with the bond of marriage between a husband and wife: *He created it first*. All things came from *it*. This book speaks of God's design for marriage from creation. His beautiful design is complete; there is nothing missing in it. God's union between Him, one man, and one woman gives couples everything they need for optimum and complete fulfillment in the earth's realm. There is simply nothing God has made to compare with His creation of marriage, His love affair. From this tri-fold and unique bond, everything else follows as should be…procreation and God's purpose or calling for this individual couple.

This book was written so that husbands and wives will grasp these infallible truths from God's Word and embrace them fully—that God may receive glory and their marriages will be completely filled with God's original design, His love affair.

"Philosophy is the most powerful thing in the universe. The Bible says of philosophy, 'For as he thinketh in his heart, so is he' (Prov. 23:7)."

"Ideas produce philosophy.
Ideas are stronger than death."

"Nothing is yours until you discover it."

"Even if you believe a lie, you'll defend error
because it is your concept of truth.
To change it, you must have bigger and better ideas,
those that will reverse that mental damage."

"Your children are victims of ideas.
You should make sure that they get better ideas.
Destroy some bad ideas by replacing
them with good ideas."

"Books live forever. That's why God put His idea in a book."

Miles Munroe
Bob Harrison Conference 2007

MARRIAGE: GOD'S LOVE AFFAIR VS. ARRANGEMENT

Definition: God's Love Affair

God's definition of marriage is a love affair.

A love affair is a man and a woman's becoming one by loving the Lord with all of their heart, soul, and mind, more than themselves or anyone else...and loving each other more than themselves, anyone else, or any physical thing.

It is holding and cherishing those very special feelings toward one another for a lifetime. It is oneness in spirit and flesh under the love of Christ.

A love affair denotes one, oneness, one love.

You must love yourself before you can love another: Your mate is your self—one person, yourself, you.

Love is easy.

He and she flows...they flow together...as one.

Definition: Arrangement

Arrangements are marriages that are out of focus with God's truest intention for marriage. These are couples whose motives for marriage are incorrect whether they confess Jesus as their Lord or not. Though these couples maintain a general love for one another, they treat marriage as something *common* instead of what *God created it to be: special*...a love affair. They have only a contractual view of marriage, so they do not find it important to protect this specialness; they do not value it; they neglect it, and it dies. *God's design dies.*

For a lack of understanding, these couples do not love each other as *one*; therefore, they place more value on *themselves* and *others* than on each other. This goes against what the Lord teaches in Ephesians 5:25 which says, "Husbands, love your wives, even as Christ also loved the church, and gave himself for it;" also in Genesis 2:24, "Therefore shall a man leave his father and his mother, and shall cleave unto his wife: and they shall be one flesh" and in Ephesians 5:28, "So ought men to love their wives as their own bodies. He that loveth his wife loveth himself." This is what God upholds for His design for marriage. Not seeing your mate as special in the way that God views him or her is the prime instigator of grief. Men and women know innately that—physically and emotionally—they are supposed to be cherished, valued, and protected *with great desire by their mates first*. When this does not happen, this lack of beautiful love in mate support results in a "giving and taking" mentality *to protect and provide for each one's own emotional and physical support*. These people are half filled, not one, always seeking some outside fulfillment to meet that empty space, not realizing that the thing that would complete them is the mate under the same roof. This is what causes the deception behind the statement "I am in love with two people" or the declaration that people can love others on the same level that they love their mates. This is not love in this instance but lust. God's love of oneness was created for only one person. **God's love affair is created for only one person**. Neglect of a mate's specialness results in performing tasks for each other just out of duty because they have "lost those loving feelings." They are married but unsatisfied, bored, and tired.

This lack of God's love results in a two-person marriage instead of a one-person marriage as God intended. These people basically maintain their own lives, sharing in momentary highs of intimacy. Because two people will never fulfill as one, such a situation is the cause of many unwise and ungodly relationships, emptiness, and pain.

Struggle and frustration are usual companions of these relationships. These couples "*work* at" peace, happiness, and spending time together. They are constantly **trying** to "create" or "keep" love emotions. Love is hard, love is a negotiation, or love is nonexistent.

GOD'S LOVE AFFAIR VS. ARRANGEMENT

God intended marriage to be a love affair

For centuries, couples believed that an arrangement was what a marriage was supposed to be. Yet, a true marriage that God intended us to have is not based on selfish decision making and adjusting to "fit" in each other's world. Such a situation is an arrangement. God's intended marriage does not *base its merit* on fitting together the differences in gender or culture for the sake of getting along. These actions are the primary focus for couples who live in arrangements. God's love is not the motivator of arrangements; these relationships are more like a business: "You do your part, I'll do my part. Marriages are *hard work*. Let's try and make this work. If it weren't for the children, we would not be together..." There is an ample supply of logic but a lack of God's intended love—what God decreed in Genesis 2:24. God's love never operates separately within a married couple. In arrangements, someone is always losing, because if you are not willing to negotiate or compromise over that thing in life that you want, you will lose your relationship. You're constantly weighing what you will lose out on just to keep the relationship. This is fear and selfishness or self-preservation, not love, motivating this relationship.

God's love never loses; it gains...more and more. God's designs are always to give life and more abundantly. The giving of God's love *meets your needs and your spouse's needs,* so no one is at a loss. There's nothing to compromise, only give. You can't take a spiritual gift (love) and try to meet it with your own human efforts. You'll always fall short of it, because a counterfeit of love is never the real thing. Love was not born out of humanity. Love is not a human thing; it never came from man. Man never created love. Love came from God, and through Him only can real love be imparted. His love always gives and is able to because it never focuses on self. Because God is the giver of life and the "meeter" of needs, His love causes our focus to turn from ourselves and meeting our own needs to placing our needs in His care...giving us all of this room to love our mates. It is a very beautiful and giving love based on God's love covenant, which will be introduced a little later in this book.

Most couples come together with an intense "like" for one another. Before marriage, you see the person and think that he/she is the most beautiful person you have ever met. These feelings or emotions that erupt in your heart have been described by some as "being on cloud-nine." Feelings such as adoration, affection, devotion, protectiveness, extreme fondness, a love craze, etc. are beautiful emotions. Though you know little of each other, the emotions of love you feel are powerful...and should be. You want to be around them, talk with them, protect them, please them, touch them, laugh with them, get to know them, stand with them through troubles, have fun with them, and on. The person gives you goose bumps— you know what I'm talking about!

Even though you do not really know the person, you feel like you do…and it is a great feeling. Your imagination starts kicking, and before you know it, she or he is perfect in your mind. These are great emotional experiences that God meant to last the couple a lifetime because God's love will never let you grow used to each other; it is multidimensional, exciting, full, and colorful. God's love is always developing a couple and is extremely pleasing.

These emotions are very strong; couples will marry each other by them. *Those very special feelings you have for one another* are *true* emotions. They are *God-given emotions*. They are powerful because they tap into the spiritual, emotional, and physical reservoirs of a human being all at once. No other relationship in this earth's realm does this. It's a gift given only to a husband and wife. ***When these cloud-nine emotions are motivated by God's love***, not lust, ***they completely fill up** the spiritual, emotional, and physical reservoirs of a human being, fulfilling every social, survival, maternal, paternal, and primal need you can think of. The human being feels spiritually and physically complete with God and his mate in his life. God designed cloud-nine emotions to be the physical **instrument** that causes two people to become one and stay one*. Without these special feelings, two people will not become one nor remain as one.

We can now see why, when these special emotions die, people separate emotionally and physically. They turn their love affair into an arrangement. God meant it when He said that the two shall become *one*. So, that very special feeling you have for your mate or future mate is *highly important* to God—which is why He gave us *His love* to sustain these loving feelings for a lifetime.

It must be stated before proceeding that *only in Jesus Christ as Lord* can a human being be eternally complete. Whether single or married, a person **must have** Jesus Christ as the Lord of his life and love Him above everything. God created marriage *to pattern after* His relationship with Jesus and the Holy Spirit (the Trinity) and *to pattern after* the relationship between Jesus Christ and the Church, not to substitute or compete with in any way the purpose for Jesus Christ as the Lord of our lives.

Cloud-nine emotions are very important to a husband and wife's relationship because they serve a purpose derived from God's love of oneness

Oneness originates with God in the Trinity. This special love of God generates **completion**. God, Jesus, and the Holy Spirit share a love and a special union of oneness that is *unique to only them.* God, Jesus, and the Holy Spirit complete each other—they are *complete* as one. *They do not need anything outside of the Trinity to complete them.*

Again, God created marriage *to pattern after* His relationship with Jesus and the Holy Spirit (the Trinity) and *to pattern after* the relationship between Jesus Christ and the Church.

Genesis 1:26 says that God declared, "Let us make man in *our image,* after *our likeness* [the Trinity's]…" First, God made man to share in a relationship of oneness with Him—God, Jesus, and the Holy Spirit. Adam was complete in terms of operating in the love of oneness with God alone. But to carry out the purpose God had for earth, covering the world with holy

15

and eternal generations (Ps. 137:3–5), God saw that Adam needed to share in a relationship of oneness with another human being, a helper who could function in the same way that the Holy Spirit and Jesus do with God. Also, this unique person must *be* Adam just like all in the Trinity *are* God.

So, God said, "It is not good that the man should be alone; I will make for him a helper fit for him" (Gen. 2:18). Some people think that a woman's purpose as a helpmate is an indication of an individual of lesser degree and not of any significant importance—that she is just another human being common among everybody, created just to reproduce and help. This is not the emphasis of a "helper" as God meant it. In the relationship with the Trinity, God, the Holy Spirit, and Jesus all possess *distinctive functions* designed to love and help one another, *yet they are one and are of extreme importance to each other*. Their distinctive functions give them the ability to help each other.

They do not treat or see each other as a devalued or separate entity. When God looks at Jesus, He sees Himself, just as with the Holy Spirit, and vice versa. Thus, God saw that man *needed union with another human being* that matched the love union He had with Jesus and the Holy Spirit. *Adam needed to see himself* in a being of equal importance yet with a different function so that they could love and help each other, reproduce…yet still be one. To do this, God took Adam out of Adam and brought Adam back to Adam. As Adam was called *to identify* everything in the garden for what it was, discover its purpose, and name it, when Adam saw his *self* coming back to him, *he identified this person as himself* and named her "Eve," which means "woman," because *she came out of him*.

Hence, we see that outside of the Trinity alone, only two relationships enjoy this special union of completion that is oneness: God with a human being, and God with a man and his wife. Though the relationship of God with a man is "complete" in terms of Christ's being all that we need spiritually, God with man alone is incomplete to carry out God's purpose of eternal generations in the physical realm of earth. This sets apart the husband and the wife as the *only* "human-to-human" *relationship of oneness* in the earth. No other human-to-human relationship possesses this unique blessing of completion, of oneness.

This special relationship of oneness is characterized by its unique nature. **It can function *only*** to serve, protect, and please, reciprocating between *the participants bonded together* in this unique relationship. Without these characteristics, this special union cannot exist. This is where cloud-nine emotions originate…to serve, protect, and please.

This is what we see in the Trinity. When one of the Trinity is wounded, God becomes an enemy to those who would wound them, because *they are wounding Him*. To serve each other is their utmost priority. As stated before, God, Jesus, and the Holy Spirit complete each other. They are *complete* as One. *They do not need anything outside of the Trinity to complete them*. God designed this special union between a man, a woman, and Him to function the same way. God's union between Him, a man, and a woman is complete. The three *do not need* anything outside of this tri-part covenant to complete them. Even the husband's and wife's unique functions do not stand on their own and thereby minimize the importance of their love union. *Their love union* stands as of foremost importance to them,

17

their unique functions are designed to bless and strengthen their love union, not operate separately from each other. Their love is oneness. This is the purpose for God's design: to draw a man and a woman in union with Him, to create a complete love union in mankind that resembles the Trinity in the physical realm.

God created these special emotions to enable a couple to "please one another" under the banner of holiness. Again, this is the characteristic of oneness, and it mimics the Trinity. It was <u>Jesus' love for the Father</u>, to "<u>please Him</u>," that compelled Jesus to die on the cross for our sins. Pleasing the Father was greater at that moment in the Garden of Gethsemane than fulfilling His *function,* which was to restore mankind back to the Father (Matt. 26:39). Jesus said in Matthew 26:39, "O my Father, if it be possible, let this cup pass from me: nevertheless not as I will, but as thou wilt." If Jesus had been thinking of His self (selfishness) and not about pleasing God, He may not have endured the cross. But He was able to overcome those feelings because there was no selfishness in Him. And to *please Jesus* for the function He had to carry out, God supplied Him with His strength to complete the tasks before Him. <u>God, the Holy Spirit, and Jesus never leave each other by themselves or to fend for themselves.</u> **They never** disregard or count as not important their feelings and needs. All that God, Jesus, and the Holy Spirit do is please each other in holiness. That is what *love* does: It gives. It only gives, and in <u>holiness</u>. Among the Trinity, this is their only desire: to bless each other.

God is love. When God speaks, the Holy Spirit moves; when there is a need, Jesus fills it. So, we can see that cloud-nine emotions for a couple were created for <u>making each other happy and pleasing each other in the holiness of the Lord</u>. **If** one's foremost desire is pleasing his mate *in the holiness of the Lord*, his efforts of pleasure will be primed with *holiness*. This will draw his mate into a deeper relationship with Christ because Christ, or holiness, will be the primary base of all his actions. The act of *pleasing each other* in God's holiness is a selfless act—It is love. It is **God's** love, that forms trust. Trust forms oneness. God designed these special cloud-nine feelings to form "oneness." God does not create anything that is not extremely significant for its purpose.

Now with that understanding, these beautiful, cloud-nine emotions *that God created to form a love union like that among the Trinity* are extremely significant.

> **"There is no way a human being, man or woman, can be fulfilled without his or her self."**
> Louis L. Forté

It is also important to see oneness from this viewpoint: God started from *one,* Adam (and Eve), meaning that when God created Adam, Eve was in Adam. God took *a part of Adam* and made Eve. In essence, God took *Adam* out of Adam, so he immediately became half empty, and she did, too. They needed each other to be **one whole person** again. They were **two of the same person**. This is the same with the Trinity; their functions merge to form one. Independently, they are not whole beings who could function as *the Trinity* on their own. If it were so, there would be no need for there to be Jesus or the Holy Spirit. God, the Father, would be enough. This is why if a man tells his mate that he is complete without her or does not need her, he is in error. The same is true of the wife. God would not have made them to mirror the Trinity if it were true that the spouse were

19

not needed. God gave woman back to Adam to return them to their original state of "oneness." Marriage is one person—the male gender *of the person* and the female gender *of the person*—but manifested in two distinct people. That's why *in a God relationship*, one plus one equals ONE. The man and the woman are ONE. **When you look at your spouse, he or she represents everything God took out of you.** That is why you need each other. As a husband, your wife completes you to live out the original plan God began in the Garden of Eden...one man and one woman. **When you look at her, you see you; when you look at him, you see you**- *weaknesses, strengths, etc.* Just like *you* should seek to become more like Christ, letting Him change your weaknesses into strengths, you should have the same heart for your spouse, *in the loving patience that God has for you.* There is only oneness. There is no "yours" or "mine," only "ours." There is no selfishness, because how can you be selfish against your own self? "I" does not exist, only "we." **Your mate *is you*. And you *are your mate*.** *How can you treat yourself badly? How can you smother your own self or tell yourself to give you space? How can you not value yourself? How can you not value your uniqueness or rarity? How can you not praise what God has given you? How can you treat yourself rudely or unfairly? How can you be dishonest with yourself? How can you make others more important than your God-given rights to prioritize your mate first?* This is how God sees you when you do your mate wrong. He sees you as one.

Something else about oneness should be recognized, too. When God created Adam, he made him a *perfect* man; this is of great importance. Adam was ***perfect*** in his physical makeup, and he was *a man without sin*. With this, God gave him *the entire world*. Adam, perfect in all his state, *lacked nothing in the entire universe*. He needed nothing...or so you would think. He had it all. Everything a man could ever desire, work towards, or ask for, <u>he had</u>. He could have done all of the fishing, golfing, traveling…anything he wanted to do. He had God's love…he had the whole world…he was perfect… Nevertheless, <u>when God Himself</u> looked upon Adam, *He saw that Adam was unfulfilled*. This makes you take a second look at your own life **if you were perfect**…having all of the things you desire or work towards…a perfect body, good looks, a perfect personality, the perfect job, status as a recognized leader in the community (rather, the whole world)…and recognize that if you had them…if you had it all…*you would be unfulfilled*. Adam had everything but was empty. Even if God had made children, friends, and family for Adam, Adam still would have been unfulfilled; God would have given these to Adam *if they would have fulfilled him,* <u>but He did not</u>.

None of these things, including the whole wide world, fulfilled Adam. <u>None of these things gave Adam what he truly needed</u>. God saw that what Adam *truly needed* <u>was a being like no other</u> to understand him and love him in a way that no one or nothing else could…**to know him intimately** in an intimacy that mimics the Trinity's. Eve became Adam's intimate part—his true fulfillment—his self. Eve became *God's absolute best gift to man, because in addition to her knowing Adam intimately, she was Adam. Now, their relationship was special, which mirrored the special, intimate relationship between God, Jesus, and the Holy Spirit, and also God's gift to mankind, Jesus.*

"When God sent Jesus to die on the cross for mankind, it was impossible for even Him to give a better gift, because He gave Himself."
Louis L. Forté

This is why Eve was perfect for Adam; she was his self. God gave Adam the *best gift*, Adam's self. This is why a wife comes with all of the features a man would ever need in a lifetime (and vice versa). She is custom made for him and he for her. ***God took out of Adam the attributes Eve needed to fulfill God's purpose as the female gender of Adam and left in Adam the attributes to fulfill God's purpose as the male gender of Eve.*** As a wife, when you see your husband, you should see the male gender of *yourself*; likewise, as a husband, when you see your wife, you should see the female gender of *yourself.*

Just like a custom car with all of the kits and accessories that luxury can buy to make a man proud...or all of the friends a man has to make him feel strong...a wife has accessories that no one in the whole world has (and same for the husband to the wife). This alone makes her more valuable, more special, than anyone or anything in the universe besides God Himself. *The entire world cannot touch her*. She is just that powerful. Proverbs says, "Who can find a virtuous woman? For her price is *far* above rubies. ... She openeth her mouth with *wisdom*; and in her tongue is the law of kindness. ... The heart of her husband doth safely trust in her, so that he have no need of spoil [loss]. ... She will do him good and not evil *all* the days of her life. ... Give her of the fruit of her hands; and let her own works praise her in the gates" (Prov. 31:10–31). **She is God's best gift to a man** (Prov. 18:22). Without her, man would have no life; without a man, she would have no life. Man was given the whole world, but it was meaningless; in addition to God, a wife gives him his reason for living. Now, one could try to substitute others or other things for a reason to live, but these will not match your mate. God set this up His way. We cannot improve on His best. This makes you again ask the question, "Why would you treat others better than her?" Why would you

22

disrespect her or choose even your children, mother, father, brothers, sisters, or friends over her? How could you compare your love of anything or anyone else with the love you should have for her or give them what rightfully belongs to her? *Her love* stands alone, *his love* stands alone. … This is how God sees it, because He gave it thus.

**"When one half of your body is hurting,
THERE IS NO WAY for the other half to be fulfilled.
*There's no way you can do your mate wrong
and be fulfilled. NO WAY."***
Louis L. Forté

Your future husband or wife, or the husband or wife you already have, is custom made for you: This needs to sink in. He or she is *built for your complete* enjoyment, fulfillment, excitement, pleasure, friendship, fellowship, family, business, ecstasy, etc. Anything that you can love on this earth—your mate's love and importance outweigh it with no match. He or she *has everything you could ever desire or need,* a complete package. If he or she were all you had in the world, you would be complete. God and God alone gives the best gifts. This is worth repeating. There is nothing that earthly life necessitates that he or she does not already have. She alone *is* extracurricular activities, she *is* fellowship, she *is* business, she *is* sports, she *is* children, she *is* family, etc.—and vice versa. There is nothing extraneous that is *necessary* for you to have; again, there is nothing that is *necessary* for you to have. **<u>Except God alone, your mate is everything that you really do need</u>**. You should never compare any want you may have with your mate.

**"God's love transforms normal life into experiences of ecstasy. When husbands and wives love each other this way,
it's easy to give themselves to each other because <u>they are giving themselves to love</u>.
Nothing, <u>absolutely nothing</u>, is greater than giving your self to God's love."**
Louis L. Forté

It is God's love that causes a couple to realize this insight, allowing them to love each other more than anyone or anything else in the earth's realm. Having this insight makes a couple's life *extremely easy* in their participation in community and social life, which is the way God meant for it to be…life as a love affair. They are able to work, raise a family, and participate in the community without ever losing those special feelings for one another for a lifetime.

**"You can put value
Only up to the degree
of your understanding of a thing…
(a WIFE, or a HUSBAND)
how much value do you put on a *diamond?*"**
Louis L. Forté

This realization also creates a powerful bond between them that *no one can break,* which follows the scripture in Matthew 19:6, "Wherefore they are no more twain, but one flesh. What therefore God hath joined together, let not man put asunder."

It is amazing to watch people actually live a love affair when they first meet, then *choose* to live miserably when they originally experienced such a good relationship. This is very perplexing when you fully realize that walking out of a love affair is not only out of God's will but does not make sense. They had no problem putting the desires and needs of their mates first when they shared those special feelings for one another. Actually, they enjoyed doing so, and very much. The man was so happy to see that smile on his fiancée's face when he bought her those red roses; she felt so wonderful to hear her fiancé brag about her to his friends. Why stop? Why choose misery, boredom, and breaking up?

> **"If you invest in stocks or real estate and you do it wisely, you're going to have a lot of money. If you invest in your husband's or wife's desires, and you do so in the love and holiness of the Lord, you <u>are going to have a lot of love</u>...a beautiful...loving.... love affair."**
> Louis L. Forté

Just the sound of a "love affair" is beautiful. What a wonderful affair, sweet as honey. You simply cannot experience any physical relationship tantamount to God's marriage—not with children, family, or friends. The love experienced in a love affair holds its own.

> **"When you have the <u>best life</u> in the earth's realm And <u>heaven waiting in the wings</u>... you have nothing to lose. *When you've got a good-enough reason,***

you can do anything."
Louis L. Forté

Only God's design for a love affair makes sense.

Arrangements

So why, then, do these beautiful emotions not last between couples? Why do the husband and wife not put each other first in the most beautiful way? One simple reason: They are not secured by a lasting foundation.

It is from a lack of understanding and a lack of God's intended love that people choose an arrangement over a love affair. God says in Hosea 4:6, "My people are destroyed for a lack of knowledge…" When one enters a relationship on a foundation of half-truths or untruths, love is not its foundation. Love is truth, God is truth, and God is love.

"When you establish a life-long system not based on God's design, truth becomes your greatest enemy."
Louis L. Forté

Again, it is amazing how couples would choose to rather live a war affair than a love affair. Love affairs are definitely easier and more fun, but many people would rather choose to live life mired in difficulty. It really does not make sense. **Sometimes, we just have to change**.

Most arrangements are built upon weapons of mass destruction: S.S.S.P., or selfishness, self-will, self-righteousness, and pride. The reason for this is that when you see your mate as common, those special and motivating feelings you had for your mate become unimportant. You do not see them as a priority the way that God wants you to see them. These beautiful feelings contained God Himself because He created them to draw you and your mate together as one. When these special feelings die, God dies in that area of your relationship. Where God is dead, pride abounds. Only in oneness is there humility *to put the other first*. In two-ness, it just feels natural to meet your own needs first because the flesh is ruling. Therefore, the only things left are these weapons of mass destruction. The beautiful, special emotions you held for your mate were God's instrument in causing you to become one with your mate, and now these emotions are dead. You do not care anymore. You do not want her or him anymore. You do not want the relationship anymore. Without God, His love, and His emotions, you have no reason now to do *anything* for your mate. Selfishness becomes extremely easy. If you cannot have your way, you would rather leave the relationship or blame each other. Why protect her, since you do not value her anymore? Why speak kindly if he now means nothing? Without these special feelings and foremost value for one another, you have no reason to put each other first anymore, and your own wants begin to take over. Putting yourself and others first, which is selfishness, becomes valued more than what God designed in your putting your mate's needs first.

"For God to love us, Jesus *had to die*. For us to love our mates, our selfishness, self-will, self-righteousness, and pride must die (Gal. 2:20).

If these don't die in you, you will never love your mate."
Louis L. Forté

Loving your mate will always *cost* you something, just like God's love for mankind cost Him something: Jesus. It will cost you to eradicate these weapons of mass destruction so that they will not destroy your special feelings for your mate. The only way to remove these weapons is dying to your flesh daily by surrendering to the Holy Spirit and to God's Word while submitting to Jesus Christ as your Lord. Romans 8:13–14 says, "For if you live according to the flesh, you will die, but if by the Spirit you put to death the deeds of the body, you will live. For as many as are led by the Spirit of God, these are the sons of God." This is why it is important to worship the Lord and only the Lord in *all* that you do. This is in every decision for you and for your relationship. This is the only way. Couples are not to worship each other but the Lord *who causes them to love each other as one. The main motivation in marriage should be God's glory.*

The love covenant changes an arrangement to a love affair

To eradicate this mindset of an arrangement, the love covenant must be invoked. It is said that "God's love will find a way." This is true because His love will free you to look, compel you to find, motivate you to stay excited, humble you *to first look at yourself, and show you how to please your mate above measure. God's love* has more pleasure in saying "we" rather than "I." It finds more pleasure in *building up your mate* than considering your own life or others. True marriage is *all about* giving. We know that the Lord is the ultimate fulfiller of human life. Without Him in our life, we will never be fulfilled. Along with Himself, He gave us our mates as physical gifts to meet the rest of our needs in a relationship. In this way, with God and your mate, you become totally complete.

God can and will change an arrangement into a love affair. His love is exponentially powerful enough to return those special feelings you once had for your mate, or future mate, in placing the proper priority on them. The answer is found in the **love covenant:**

Love Covenant

- *Love the Lord thy God* **with all thy might, thy soul, and thy mind.**
- *Love the Lord more than* **you do yourself and others.**
- *Love your mate more than* **you do yourself and *more than* any other person or physical thing or activity.**

Louis L. Forté

Loving Your Mate

God constructed no other relationship as more important than the bond between a husband and wife. As our Father, *He wants husbands and wives to imitate the love that He has for us between themselves. The love in a true marriage will look like God's*: the love of Jesus for the church, His bride. Therefore, when mates love each other more than they love themselves, anyone, or anything else in this physical world, they are expressing the love of God. Marriage now becomes a love affair, as they now are flowing in the rhythm of God.

In love, there are unlimited blessings: anticipation, happiness, ecstasy, peace, etc. There is no end to love. Love grows deeper and stronger. Better and better. Without God, having a love affair is impossible because God created it. God is able to do exceedingly and abundantly above all that we can ever ask or think, according to His power that works in us (Eph.1:19–20).

> **"Marriage in action is a love affair lived out.**
> **A love affair demonstrated**
> **is a love affair manifested in the physical**
> **and spiritual realm."**
> Louis L. Forté

After a couple creates this basic foundation for marriage, each one needs to genuinely love the other with all of his/her heart; literally, to be consumed by each other's love. This consuming by each other would signify that "there is nothing between you, God, and me. All of me belongs to you on any given day to do as you want since I am in your care (and vice versa)." This is why a couple must maintain the basic foundation mentioned above because you are actually *giving yourself to the other **not out of duty but out of intense desire***. When couples give themselves to each other like this, they are giving themselves to God's love. You can see that without God's leading, this would be impossible.

Having a love affair is to love someone so passionately that even things you do not like to do you will do with no problem, meaning that it will not be a negative issue or grudging sacrifice to you. You will do these things with each other with the same excitement as if you meant to do them. It will be just a *change* in excitement, not a restriction or downgraded feeling. Loving your mate is not making sacrifices for them but doing things out of enjoyment and happiness, whether it is changing your behavior, doing something a bit differently just to please them, perhaps adjusting not what you say but how you say it. … Each mate needs something from the other to feel complete and loved by them. *The tenderness and protectiveness in a love affair will open the secrets of heart, allowing each mate to share in each other's private world without risk of abandonment or regret. God's love encompasses their most precious revelations to each other, allowing them to share in each other's life protected and as one.*

"An arrangement is an <u>unsafe</u> environment.
In an unsafe environment, YOU CAN NEVER BE
ALL THAT YOU CAN BE!
(YOU ARE RESTRICTED!)"
Charlie Briggs

"But in a love affair, you're in a safe environment
to be ALL that you can be

...because you ARE FREE!"
Louis L. Forté

*Your love and excitement **for each other** must be greater than any of your own physical enjoyments.* Just to be with each other should outweigh any other physical thing you could do, even over the enjoyment of an outside person—a friend or family member, etc. Each person should be excited to be with each other. **Though they participate in life surrounding them, they do not *need any*thing else in the physical dimension to be at their best, content, or happy.** For example, purchasing that home or car you have always been waiting for, or winning the lottery, or even having a child...all of these excitements about being fulfilled, happy, etc. are not to be compared with the feelings for your mate. He or she should be more important than anything in the world.

Being compassionate, excited, and *grateful* for what God made for you in your mate is the only way to truly live. It is God's will for married couples to spend time together, go places together, communicate, play, touch, embrace, and be intimate with one another. Everything that God desires for us He created to be enjoyed to the fullest. That is what makes life beautiful. This is God's harmony or rhythm for a love affair.

Who marries in order to be angry, separate, sleep on the edge of the bed, or not touch each other? Who wants to lose *those so-important* "loving feelings"? God's gifts are superior. Allow your special feelings towards your mate to catapult your relationship higher and higher. *Nobody else's needs should compete with your mate's nor take up residence in your heart. Let your heart be singled out for God and your mate alone.*

32

Then, you can take on life, raise a family, and fulfill the excitement of your dreams.

Ideas Learned about Marriage

Psychology shows how powerful ideas are: how each one of us learns ideas, then believes them, then lives them, and, at last, becomes them. Just imagine a little child seeing, learning, and absorbing his parents' arrangement versus a love affair. As the child becomes an adult, his learning becomes his reality; whether he saw love, indifference, or abuse, he was taught a love affair or an arrangement. Just for someone to pause a moment and *recognize* what he has learned, to look internally and see what his reality is now in comparison to the pattern seen as a child, **is a powerful step—*a destiny step.*** Once one is honest about what he has become and compares it to the love affair God purposed, ***humility*** now stands at the door and knocks. *Open the door and allow the Holy Spirit to come in and change what was learned into God's design for a love affair.* We cannot do this by ourselves. It takes the power of the Holy Spirit and our honesty; otherwise, we will be in a constant fight with ourselves.

So, was it a love affair you learned from your parents or a war affair? Maybe it was no affair. Is everything you are doing now in your relationship *for your mate or future mate*, or is it for yourself and everyone else? Just based on the *ideas implanted* in our heads as children, it is no wonder why God commands us to die to the flesh daily (Rom. 8:13–14), to allow His Holy Spirit to lead and change us in His love. To see things His way, *we have to change our ideas to His ideas.* We can do this only by *replacing* what we have learned with what He wants for us. Learning to live in God's love affair is very important because the death caused by living outside of God's love affair is real. Stories abound of those who have died emotionally due to the lack of God's love in their arrangement—and then physically took their lives. God's love in a couple's relationship is powerful. A lack of God's love has powerful repercussions. Emotions are very strong. We were not created to suppress them or think that we are strong enough not to consider them. God gave them to us to make life meaningful and to cause us to enjoy life in Jesus. ***Emotions are protected, built up, and matured in a well-balanced, healthy way when there is a love affair. Emotions will always be unbalanced, deficient, and needy in an arrangement. Emotions are too strong for the flesh to deal with. Man is a spirit; emotions are spiritual. It takes the Holy Spirit, the God who created the spirit, to change the emotional nature of a man to line up with His character of love.*** Romans 5:5 promises that "the love of God is shed abroad in our hearts by the Holy Ghost which is given unto us."

"No logic or psychological understanding can change an emotion to God's love. Only God can."
Deborah L. Rivera

Love can come only from God because—and it is worth repeating—God is the master of love. Anything less will fail. We see it every day. Men, women, teens, boys, and girls are dying due to a lack of love they have seen between their parents. No matter how handsome you are…how beautiful you are…how intelligent, athletic, or rich…you will live life unfulfilled if you choose to live without the love that God intended to be in your heart for your mate.

There may be someone you know who took his own life or emotionally died from a broken heart. This was never God's plan. We all are born into this life, and we will leave this life. Is God's intended love attached to the method of life you are living now in your marriage or with your future mate?

A Love Affair: Parents' Greatest Gift to Their Children

"It is a wonderful thing for children to see their parents live a love affair and grow up into adults with a blueprint now built within them for a love affair for themselves."
Louis L. Forté

This was God's original design **to pass His love of oneness through the generations**. God design was for perfect husbands and wives to have dominion over and replenish the earth *with more perfect husbands and wives, all living in God's love affair and bringing forth God's will*. God designed husbands and wives, not children, specifically for earthly living. Children are just a byproduct in transit to becoming husband and wives. As it states in Psalm 127:3–5, "Lo, children are an heritage *of the* LORD: and the fruit of the womb is *his* reward ..." God says that children are His reward, not ours. The passage continues:

"As arrows are in the hand of a mighty man; so are children of the youth. Happy is the man that hath his quiver full of them: they shall not be ashamed, but they shall speak with the enemies in the gate." The word "happy" is not referring to a satisfaction or fulfillment that matches, is like, or equals the satisfaction or fulfillment of a mate. The purpose and meaning for having a mate and having children are separate and unique. Dake's Annotated Reference Bible states of Psalm 127:3,

> "Eternal coming generations of natural people on earth will be the reward God is looking for...God created the earth and other planets to be inhabited (Isa. 45:18).He also will see to it that those who live eternally in control of His creations are righteous and free from all possibility of rebellion (I Cor. 15:24–28: Eph. 1:10; Rev. 21:3–7; 22:3).This verse refers to the original and eternal law of reproduction of man (v3; Gen.1:26–28; 8:22;9:12; Isa. 9:6–7; 59:21; Dan. 2:44–45; 7:13–14, 27; Lk. 1:32–33; Rev. 11:15; 22:4–5)."[1]

In reference to verses 4 and 5, it says,

> "Each child will, in the process of time, be a defense, support, and propagation of the eternal reproduction of man and the fulfillment of the plan of God for man—as arrows in the hand of a mighty man. The more arrows one has[,] the more enemies he may slay, and the more powerful he will be in the earth. The more children born and saved to help God administer the affairs of the

[1] From *Dake's Annotated Reference Bible* (p. 1012, Psalms 127:3(a) and p. 1059 – Eternal Generations), by Finis Jennings Dake, 1999, Lawrenceville, Georgia: Dake Publishing. Copyright 1999. Used with permission.

eternal plan for man, the more reward <u>God</u> will have (v4)."[2]

We see here that the personal joy in your children or the personal joy in having children should not be because they belong to you *but rather* be a joy that God has given you the task of guiding them in Him, for Him, and for His purposes. Your Godly upbringing—your teaching them His Word, teaching them *that they do not belong to you and that they belong to God for a purpose He has predestined*—will be to fulfill His purpose for eternal generations. The joy of children also, as referenced to above, should be because it blesses the building up of your house and adds to your household a defense. Your joy should come because the Lord is pleased by your obedience to Him in how you raise them, not because you have a smaller "you" – it's not about you. Every couple should hold a special love for their children, because *they are precious, and yes, we do love them very much*; but we are to see them as precious *as the Lord would have us to, not in our own way.*

In today's society, this is not the view that husbands and wives have toward their children. Their view of children is cherished on the same level as having a wife or a husband—"family is family"—but the purpose for each could not be further apart. This makes one take note that if God made different purposes, creations, and designs of a husband and wife and children, the way that we view children and relate to them in our daily lives should be different. The personal joy over your child should never match or supersede the joy over your mate because ***God put an order of importance*** on the task each is created for, and we must follow His pattern.

---

[2] Finis Jennings Dake, *Dakes Annotated Reference Bible*, p.1012 Psalms 127:4(b), 5(c)

Ephesians 5:25 never told **husbands** to love their **children** as Christ loved the Church, but rather their wives. Though we are to love our children, it is in perspective of *teaching them the love of God according to **His design**,* which is God's way of doing things, and His perspective of love in the home (Prov. 22:6). Though it says in Titus 2:4 to "...teach the young women to be sober, to love their husbands, to love their children...," the love given to the husband versus the love given to the children must be different in order to agree with Luke 16:13, which says, "No servant can serve two masters: for either he will hate the one, and love the other; or else he will hold to the one, and despise the other." Putting the same priority on the husband (or wife) as on the child makes the adult and the child equal in status and seniority in the home, giving this home two masters. The Bible is clear that you cannot serve two masters—the love will not be the same. One will have seniority. God's Word is clear: Our happiness and love for our children stem from raising them in the way they should go, which is *for them to learn that they belong to God* and to *fulfill His purpose* as He shows it forth in His Word.

When family is just family, everyone is on the same level of importance; this is where inordinate bonding within the family unit, dividing the mates, can occur.

This can be seen clearly in the "special" relationships that *tradition and society* have set up in the family like father-daughter and mother-son. *None of these were set up or ordained by God.* They do not adhere to *His design* for marriage and **_His reason_** for children. Children should not believe that they have something special with one parent of an importance that *outweighs, equals,* or *has merit to challenge* the husband-wife relationship. No daughter should ever feel that her importance outweighs her mother's, nor should the son his father's. No child should be taught that *his/her place* is beside the father/mother. Children should be taught that their father and mother are ONE—that the child is not daddy's girl or mommy's boy but rather '*daddy and mommy's*' girl and '*daddy and mommy's*' boy. It may seem trivial, but it is a subliminal teaching of division and a subliminal teaching of a false "specialness" that is on the *same level as*, or is *very close to*, the marriage bond itself. You can tell if this is so by just the way you "*need*" or "*respond*" to your mate versus to your children. If the first priority on your mind is your children, if they are the ones who bring you the most joy in your life, if they are the most special to you, if you feel this special closeness *primarily* to them, or if they are the ones who receive the *predominance* of your thoughts and protection, they are more important to you than your mate. This is why children have a hard time differentiating who is more important in the home. *When you teach your children that they are of equal value to you as your mate is, that you CAN and WOULD divorce your mate but NOT THEM, and that they have something special with you UNLIKE your mate, you have told the children that THEY HAVE CERTAIN INNATE AND ATHORITATIVE RIGHTS MORE VALUABLE THAN YOUR MATE's. Whatever is more special to you, you will never leave or forsake. You will stick with them through whatever situations you encounter. Doesn't society applaud loving the parent-child relationship over the marriage relationship? You can leave and stop loving your mate, but you NEVER leave nor stop loving your children. Yet what does God say about this?*

God's instruction/design is completely opposite. God *hates* divorce *between husband and wife, because they are **one** with Him; yet He instructs a permanent separation between children* _and parents_ because _children belong to Him separately_ and are not part of the covenant union between Him, the husband, and the wife. Nevertheless, society teaches the total opposite—that you should divorce your mate with your union with God but never separate from your children. Society teaches that your children should see your relationship with them as number one instead of teaching them that the number-one relationship they should have is with God and that their parents' relationship between each other **alone** is _paramount_ in the eyes of the Lord. **This is so terribly backwards and works completely against what God is trying to do and what He designed.**

By teaching children that their relationship with you is unbreakable and your relationship with your mate is breakable, you taught that their relationship with you is much stronger. You have just taught them a lie. This can create the need in children to act out the role of a wife or husband to the mate, competing with the other mate, and this can start at a very early age when they are not taught otherwise. James 3:16 says, **_"For where envying and strife is, there is confusion and every evil work,"_** which many times will create unnatural affections between parent and child or unnatural rights between parent and child, whether sexual or immoral or just a relationship that comes _first_ in your life, placing your marriage in the background. From the child's perspective, the chosen parent comes first rather than God in his or her life **and** _valuing their parents as one._ The child is taught or allowed to pick a favorite between the parents. This is not God's design. Children should be taught that they could never have a special relationship with one parent over the other. How can you separate one person? How could a child say, "I hate Mom and love Dad" or "I hate Dad and love Mom" if both parents are _operating_ **as one** and loving the children **in the love of the Lord**, _not from their own_ *feelings*? How could a child be jealous of one parent's attention if the child is taught that certain rights belong to the husband and wife and that the attention they are seeking *is not their place*?

To tell your children that *you both, **as one**,* love them and will spend appropriate time with them as *a husband and wife team,* it will set the stage of God's plan. You are teaching them His wisdom, not what the children feel like they should have, not what you as parents feel like they should have, or what society says that they should have, but what *God says* is what they should be taught. Now, seeing God's genuine love between their parents, they will believe what you tell them and look forward to becoming one with their future mates. **This matures a child**. *It gives them a reason for why you are drawing these God-ordained love boundaries and not just rejecting them for an unreasonable request.* God gets involved. You now have His divine help, for He is always present and faithful to fulfill His plans, His designs. Instead of throwing tantrums and being selfishly taught from unaware parents, children are being put in the presence of the Lord, in His power and His will; and wherever His will is being applied, He is faithful to finish what He starts. It is through His divine power that He matures His little ones. Our job is to obey and trust Him, not lead from our own understanding (Prov. 3:5). Since our children belong to God, it will take being in His will to raise them.

If children and teens are used to seeing **_you both_** spend time with them *together **as one**,* rather than each taking turns, trying to build separately from one another, they will have an early image of what God's design is. There is strength in togetherness, a weakening and an opportunity for competition and attack in separateness. It should be stated too that this applies to married couples who have children from a previous marriage. By operating *as one*, the husband and the wife would always *protect the position of oneness—**each other**, and loving their children together for God's purposes, **not their own***. This love that the parents give their children will look like God's because it will be His, not their own conception or their own vicarious needs, likes, or dislikes. Their own conception could be anything, but God's will be based in *holiness* (1 Pet. 1:15–17), His **wisdom** (Prov. 22:6), and His love, *which follows fruit of the Spirit, "But the fruit of the Spirit is love, joy, peace, lonsgsuffering, gentleness, goodness, faith, meekness, temperance…"* (Gal. 5:22–23).The boundaries and intentions of love in a home with God's Word will be clear and honorable. [Note: Wisdom here is in bold letters because many times, parents have good intentions to try to love their children in holiness and in God's love but will *mistakenly **disregard** God's wisdom*. They as parents will ***act*** unwise, ***allow*** unwise decisions to rule the home, or ***let*** their children behave in a certain way that is not good, considering it as "normal." Or, again, parents will *separately build* a unique union with their child, creating a stronger single parent-child bond than the husband-wife bond. This is unwise because it is fortifying bonds that are against the love bonds God is trying to build. As long as Satan can give a counterfeit, the real thing will never be experienced. A counterfeit will always attempt to steal the place of the genuine article—God's love between a man and a woman could never be matched or compared to any other relationship, including with children. Satan wants us to miss that.]

In God's wisdom and love are unity and order. He designed His love to have a hierarchical system in the family unit so that it will function and produce His design for oneness and holy eternal generations. The hierarchal separateness God commands between the husband-wife unit and the children is not to break His love in the family *but how to apply it*. His instructions define the boundaries of how He wants His love to flow and be taught within the family unit. It is just like how God defined the love between the husband and wife in the love covenant. Though His love is to flow through both of them for each other, *there is a way in which He wants this done*. He commands a hierarchal love position: Jesus is the head of the marriage, the man is in the lead position between him and his wife, the wife is the lesser between her and her husband, and the husband and wife as one are the lead over their children. Here, God's order in His love of oneness is established. There just cannot be love in a relationship *given any way one pleases…* if so, **a counterfeit emerges**. *Anything outside God's love, <u>results in a changing</u> from His love.* What God does not create, works against His design – or one could say, if God did not change what He has created, then *He hasn't approved* any changes man has done to His creations. This is why to love your child or a family member with the affections of a mate is incest; to love an animal like a mate is bestiality; and to bring two people as mates other than a man and a woman all deviate from what He created. All of these forms of lust that man changed from God's love, God said are an abomination to Him because they change *His truth* into *a lie* (Lev 20:11-21). When Jesus died on the cross for our sins, He did not do away with God's law but fulfilled it. **Only one can be right – <u>God's law or man's ideas-</u>** <u>*one is the truth, the other is a lie…both cannot be true, because the statements of God completely go against all the deviations of man*</u>. To prove God is wrong, and that man is free to love how he wants and who he wants, one would have to prove that God is a liar. In order to challenge Him, is to prove that He is wrong. But to truly do that, one would have to be like Him, all-knowing, all-powerful, eternal – exists before and after our creation and death, this person must *be truth* – not a form of it; because *any deviation* from the truth *is a lie*. *This man must be as God is and cannot die*. If he dies, he is mortal and helpless, and his ideas of truth have died with him because he cannot enforce them. What man has all of these abilities to prove God wrong? How can the finite change what the infinite has established? What man *is* *truth* to prove God wrong? Who has ever been eternal, involved in the creation of man? What man will be with you after you die, **who** will be **able to defend you** before God – to tell God, who has all power over life and death, heaven and hell, that He is a liar and that man's ideas are true and not His? **To tell Him what His love is**; that *your beliefs of His love is the truth* and what He says doesn't matter? **God says He is the first and the last, the beginning and the end** (Rev 22:13), and that **He is the way, the truth, and the life** (Jn 14:6). Does any man dare make those claims, and not die to prove it? Romans 3:4 says, "…let God be true, and every man a liar." Truth never dies; it is not mortal; *truth is eternal*. Truth was at our beginning, and will complete our ending. Imagine a child telling his parents and everyone else that he was not birthed by his parents (when he was); or like the model of a car telling its manufacturer XYZ Co., "You didn't make me – I'm a CST Co. car!" Seems ludicrous doesn't it, this is exactly what is done when men change God's designs to fit their own wants and lusts, and say that God approves of it, yet…He never has. God is the same, yesterday, today and forever (Rev 22:13), and He says in Rev 22:18-19,

> "For I testify unto every man that heareth the words of the prophecy of this book, If any man shall add unto these things, God shall add unto him the plagues that are written in this book: And if any man shall take away from the words of the book of this prophecy, God shall take

away his part out of the book of life, and out of the holy city, and from the things which are written in this book."

It sounds harsh, but God is just…He makes the rules of the universe just as our courts try to be just and make the rules over the land, and parents try to be just making rules for their children…all of which at times can seem harsh. But love is discipline; it is "rules"; it has boundaries; it is not just anything and everything to please someone. The rules of our courts are designed not to harm each other, even more so our God of the universe. He wants nothing but love for us and between us. *God is love*…who are we to change Him? – His rules in His court? **(Sometimes, we just *have* to change. "Dear Lord, teach us to number our days that we may apply our hearts to wisdom" [Ps 90:12]).**

In God's hierarchal positioning, we see a separation of love boundaries to establish His order: His wisdom. His love boundaries do not take away or degrade His love but establish it: *Without His order, it wouldn't be **His love***. His love has life; anything other than His love is death. His love boundaries are needed for a fertilized ground for His love to exist and grow. This is His reason for the love boundaries He calls for between the husband-wife unit and the children. It establishes a unique and special period of separation unto Him when there is great need in the children's life to spend time with Him personally in prayer, to learn to trust His faithfulness, and to learn of His power and love. *God becomes first place* in the child's life, which is where God wants to be so that He can mature this child and give this child wisdom to live the life He predestined, *like a beautiful incubation period all to the Lord*. This is why it is necessary to give the child that little push away from the parents. If the children are taught that they belong to their

45

parents and that their dependence is on their parents, they won't know that they belong to God, and they won't learn to depend on Him.

God's hierarchal love boundaries create this special place between Him and the children (or teens) so that they may know each other intimately. This is training and mentorship before they must go out and fulfill their call or gift God has for their lives. It could be compared to an eagle and its babies. The eagle pushes the little ones away from itself to teach them to depend on another and to discover life for themselves. When you think of the sunset, there is God's heavenly portrait...created upon *His order*. Even the loveliest piece of music contains an *order* of notes that builds into a crescendo of harmony. If God thought it best to see that "how" things are done is important, shouldn't we? Especially when handling *His* creations, not ours? **For everything God creates, *His order* is to bring about His glory**.

With so much of society teaching that parents should be best friends with their children, have we allowed our children to have attitudes and behave like they are on the same level as their parents? This commonality does not teach them the importance of God's hierarchal system of love nor *the place that belongs to the mates*. When children, teens, and young adults are allowed to flow in and out of the special place God designed only for mates, confusion arises. *For, even as children, teens, etc., they are either building or destroying God's design; they can't do both.* Again, ***there is a place*** allotted <u>to your mate that belongs only to them</u>. Even if a mate is wrong in a decision at times, you should never let the child believes he or she has the upper hand over the mate. We are to speak the truth about the error – do not cover it up; *yet still hold and command the*

46

respect and position of your mate as the situation is dealt with by the Word of God and through prayer.

When "this place" that belongs to the mates is taught to the children through word and behavior, it will make it easy for the children to see a clear example of how to relate to their parents. The level of honor and dignity towards their parents will be there because the children will see how each parent puts this position of authority and respect on each other and commands it from those in training...the children.

What belongs to the wife is the wife's, not the daughter's. What belongs to the husband is the husband's, not the son's. This encompasses specialness, attention, behavior, time, respect, honor, priority, thought life, and that special, tender place. When a **husband** looks at **their** daughter and has that special feeling towards her that he has *for no one else,* that cherishing, unique, tender, and only special place of his heart, he has just given her what belongs to *his wife*. The same applies to a wife regarding the son.

What is unfortunate is that many do this not purposely but unaware. Most people have not been taught socially or through their family that this unique, tender, and most special place belongs **only** to their mate. When this place is not given to the other mate, the children pick up on it immediately, and they know that they are more special than their mother or father. Not only so, but it cannot be stressed enough that *the wife is just a little girl*—with all of the cuteness, sweetness, and charm that a two-, five-, or ten-year-old has…and again, what is so remarkably true, **is that she really is!***(and vice versa).* Every one of us **is** the child in us, regardless of age. What one goes through from the time he takes his first breath is special and always childlike. Adults still have the same childlike feelings they held when they were children; they are just more knowledgeable now. The child in us never goes away, so when a wife or husband looks at her or his mate, shouldn't it be with that affection that society incorrectly insists that the daughter or son should *uniquely* have with that parent?

Let's go a little further. What if the husband looked at and treated his wife with that very special preciousness that husbands are incorrectly taught to so tenderly give their daughters while disregarding their wives? What if he gave this, and it was very real towards his wife? Could you imagine her response? ***It would be amazing!*** *You are treating her, giving her what is hers and belongs to her: being her **hero**.* And it would be real. And she, his wife, would be to him everything…a tender precious jewel that he would voraciously protect and make sure that she gets the best of life in pampering, loving, spending time with, valuing highly, treating honestly, and cherishing with the highest respect. Isn't this what society teaches husbands to do for their daughters instead of their wives? Why do husbands grow so infuriated when their daughters are mistreated, yet they will do to their wives—who are unmatchable in preciousness—equally wrong and many times *much* worse? What does this tell the children? It says very clearly that Dad has more love for the daughter than for the mother. You will fight to protect only what is most precious in your heart. No one can serve two masters. One will be served first and the other left behind. This is tragic. It is no wonder that wives do not feel that special bond or connection with their husbands. The husband's neglect and giving away what rightfully belongs to the wife has caused that specialness to die in her. ***Her beautiful inner child <u>for</u> <u>him</u> dies***. Wouldn't a husband want his most precious love in the world, his wife, to

48

feel extremely close to him, rather than regard him as something that can easily be discarded or despised? And if your wife *is* just a little girl, needing that special love, then how does she feel when you are supposed to build her, cherish her, and hold her like no one else in the world but you don't? Instead, you give that priority away to someone who doesn't belong to you—since your daughter belongs to God and her future husband—while this little girl, your wife, *is yours* and *is 'you*?'

Many parents have been taught to share this love with their children, but this is inaccurate. *Some things are valued uniquely in the design of God's creation.*

If you are supposed to have a special love for your children that you don't for your mate, how will you train your children? As a father, imagine telling your daughter, "When you grow up and get married, your husband will share a unique place with your daughter but won't love you as such. The twinkle in his eye will be for her but not for you. He may, and has a right to, leave you—but not your daughter." Or, he could say, "Honey, the Lord has someone He is preparing for you who will love you above anyone or anything. He will value you incomparably like no other above your children, friends, family, or job, and he will be with you till you both die—just like I cherish and love your mother." Which one will she want? The daughter will say, "I can't wait to have a husband who loves me like Dad loves Mom." **The *real-life example* of God's love affair from the parents is how God set it up for our children to learn, *not giving what belongs to the mates* to the children to try and teach them. Dates are for mates**. *God did not* set it up for parents to teach their children by interacting with them the way that they are supposed to interact with their mates. They are to teach by example and God's Word only. God's wisdom, His love, and His Word are enough.

Unfortunately, this is what parents are teaching their children through their spoken and body language. Fathers are *pushed* so much to spend one on one time with the daughters that this has become a primary focus. When going places, you see this regularly, where the father and daughter are close/holding hands and *the mother is off to the side* – rather than seeing *the husband and wife close/holding hands* and the children off to the side. Or, the daughter is always with the father alone, rather than honoring that place for the wife. <u>As children or teens, boys and girls should be loved, valued and cherished **equally** from their parents like our Father in heaven loves us – He does not give the woman preferential treatment; He loves the man and woman equally</u>.

God's love never puts a preference of more of His tenderness on either gender; the lack of understanding in mankind is the divider. All of mankind after Adam and Eve was born in sin (Ps. 51:5); the whole family. We did not have in our hearts to love God and hate sin. But when Jesus came and gave us victory over sin (1 Cor.15:57), the Holy Spirit then was able to pour God's love into our hearts (Rom. 5:5) that we may have a heart after God – to love what He loves and hate what He hates. That's why Jesus says He came to bring a sword. *His sword represents His love and righteousness; His sword will divide those who follow after Him and those who will not (Mat.10:34).* People get it wrong to think God wants mothers and daughters, fathers and sons to not get along just because of gender; this would make Him the author of confusion which He never could be (1 Cor.14:33). This would also go against who

He is and what He is about – **He is** the love between people, and the peace of the home (Isa.9:6).

God tells us *not to neglect* our roles *as stewards* over our children but TEACH them in the way in which they SHOULD go. Not in our way, or society's way, **but God's way**. Stewards (parents) have accountability or *a duty* to their creator (God). If children belonged to parents, the parents would have sole discretion to raise them as they please; if they want to follow the rules of man, or make up their own rules, it would be so. But God said that children are *His* heritage and that *He* created the parents as stewards to raise them to become like *He* wants them to be.

When God teaches, He does so with WISDOM. Wisdom tells you the "HOW" everyone in the home *should behave* to build oneness (the marriage covenant) and teaches the children that they belong to God. Wisdom is the "how" to speak about your mate, the "how" to protect their position of oneness in all things, "*how*" to relate to the children as a husband-wife unit, "*how*" the children are to relate to their *parents as one*, not separately. Wisdom is in the **how** *that it is done. This is extremely important.* Again, in the case of marriages with children from previous relationships, this is so extremely important because strife, competition, hatred, and emotional wounds are so prevalent. In the attempt to sometimes preserve the child's emotional balance from the wounds of brokenness from the previous marriage, the parent of this child will favor or emotionally attach stronger to this child than to their new mate. Though well intentioned to try to mend something broken, this action is out of God's order and is wrong. It is a natural human emotion to try and fix something that is broken right away and with our own human abilities. But there is no comparison between fixing something our own way versus God's way. Our way is usually focused on a quick fix and what we see and feel on a daily basis. God's way is *always the right way*, and it is based on ***faith in His Word***, which is in the confines of His love, His wisdom, and His design for life. With faith, *it may take a while and not be a quick fix* for the season of God's grace. It is in His powers of intervention to change something.

Husbands and wives are not one with their children. Husbands and wives are one with each other and ***should not treat*** their children as if they are one with them or let their children believe that they are the sole life and happiness of their parents. These motives, beliefs, and actions are inordinate. These motives and beliefs were never God's purpose; therefore, these motives should not be what drives parents to have children or drives children to inordinately bond to their parents. *When we don't understand the reason why our loving Father set forth ordinances and purposes in His creation of us and our roles and positions within the family, we will do with them any way **we** please, see them any way **we** desire, and relate to them any way that **we** see fit. This is why there are so many internal problems in the family unit because no one understands their God-given purpose, their God-given role, and the boundaries **He—not man—created***.

Second to giving children Jesus Christ as their Lord and Savior, showing children a love affair is the greatest love or gift parents can give to their children. There is no other gift that can match it. The way they see their dad treat their mom, the way they see their mom treat their dad; watching their parents love and put each other first, laughing, playing, always doing the best for each other—They will want for themselves what their parents had, *and they will believe that they can have it because it was* _real_. When we do what God says, He performs! He is faithful! The love in the home will be so beautiful: the husband and wife loving each other, then them _as one_ loving their children in God's wisdom. **_There's no comparison._**

When these children become teens and start to date, this love affair has wonderfully already become their philosophy, so it becomes easy for them to mirror it in their dating. Honoring the Lord will have a strong importance for them as they protect and put the needs of their dates first. This behavior will follow them into their engagements if nothing deters it and ultimately will blossom in their marriages. This is powerful. One life has changed. A generation has changed. (Sometimes, we just have to _change_.)

Unfortunately, many couples put their children first. Children innately know that something is out of balance or wrong with this because strife, or dissatisfaction, is always present between the parents. Many times, competition, disrespect, and strain inundate the entire family. Putting children, family, friends, or any external thing first before your mate is not God's idea of a love affair, and it is out of His rhythm of life. Anything outside of God is Satan or God's Word perverted. When you teach your children anything outside of God's design, you pervert His philosophy for life. This is why children-, family-, job-, community-, or hobby-first arrangements never fulfill the couple or the family and rarely last. They are not God's design. Neglect, seeking outside fulfillment, and unexpressed frustrations are the inhabitants of these kinds of relationships. Never will the couple or the children experience the love affair God had for them in their destiny unless God comes in and intervenes. **_This is very sad and unfortunate. There are so many broken homes all because there was no love affair_** *between the parents; there was no God for the children to see*. *God is seen only in His love*. It does not have to be this way. Everything is a choice. God holds everyone to his own personal responsibility. It cannot be stressed enough: *Everything is a choice*. God said His people are destroyed for a lack of knowledge. What you choose to do with God's intended love in your marriage as a couple and for your children is your choice. *You will end up with one or the other: God's love affair or your arrangement, which will lead to death in some area. It is your choice.*

"From Genesis to Revelation, God says: Trust Me."
Louis L. Forté

Life is a Rhythm

"Everything God does is in rhythm or harmony. When we live our lives in His rhythm, our lives are rich, fulfilled, and exciting."
Louis L. Forté

Love is the rhythm of God. Everything He does is love *because He is love.*

Love magnifies whatever it touches. Blues are bluer and sweet becomes sweeter. There is no limit to the magnification of love when it touches someone's life. God's love has the power to change anything. Love can and will change an arrangement into a love affair when we love our mates the way God wants us to—from the special love for them we have in our hearts.

In order to live in His rhythm, we must as couples live a love affair. We must live out "oneness" and do what God designed for marriage.

1. Both the man and the woman must love the Lord Jesus Christ with all of their hearts, minds, souls, and emotions more than themselves, anyone or anything else.

2. Each mate must love the other mate more than he loves himself, anyone else, or any physical thing in this world.

In God's rhythm of life, just as there is a physical rhythm—proper exercise, rest, and diet—*there is a spiritual rhythm* that is key to living in God's love affair. It is the fruit of the Spirit (Gal. 5:22–23): love, joy, peace, longsuffering, gentleness, goodness, faith, meekness, and temperance…<u>against such, there is no law</u>. This is a powerful statement. ***When you treat your mate outside of these fruits, you have no law to back it up.***

This is why it is critical for couples *to live for Christ*, not just know about Him, worshiping Him foremost in the relationship (Col. 1:15–18). For a love affair to exist, this couple must *love* God – not just know about Him. Without Him, a love affair would be impossible. Love is not intellectual or physical; it is spiritual, and it is the most powerful *force* in the universe. It is the embodiment of God; it is God. God is love. Those who think that living a love affair is a fairy tale, simply impossible, you are right. ***Without God and walking in <u>His intended</u> love towards one another as a couple, this kind of love is impossible. Love is spiritual…more than practical.*** *God could never be* what *man* says He is. God is *who* and *what* **He** says He is. God is yesterday, today, and forever. That is God, and that is more than practical. He is Alpha and Omega; that is more than practical. He raised Jesus from the dead; that is more than practical. Faith is God; faith is more than practical. Love is God; love is more than practical. God is past finding out. We just have to do what He tells us to do.

We are going to need God 100%, and we must give His love 100%. This cannot be done without humility, the Holy Spirit, and Jesus Christ as Lord of both mates. One mate cannot do this alone; it takes both of them. They must have the ***same passion*** for each other and Christ; this cannot be unequal. If they are both growing closer to Christ and putting each other first, they will never grow apart.

God's love will always build the relationship of the couple first when dealing with any matter

There is a difference couples of a love affair reflect toward God, their mate, and walking in Godly character versus what couples in arrangements reflect. Both will face the same situations, but they will view them and tackle them very differently. In God's love affair, situations are seen only as challenges to be tackled with the Word of God and His love. In an arrangement, situations are seen as problems with no solutions but to deal with them: without a solution, a situation is a problem, not a challenge. Challenges come with answers to overcome them, but problems have no solutions, so the burden of living with this problem forever causes couples to either abandon the relationship or live in such a way as to avoid the problem, neither bringing the love of God in the relationship and to each other. When God's love deals with a thing, there is always an answer, and both the man and the woman stay loving toward each other using the fruit of the Spirit. God's love is always about "change" – changing what is wrong to what is right.

The love affair couple will tackle a challenge with love, using God's Word as the mediator while still being very much "in love." Challenges are kept private, and the couple protects the dignity, character, and face value of their mates in front of family, friends, and outside parties. The love of God in them causes them to build and support one another, for each of them has the desire for the other to come out more beautiful in the sight of their network of family, friends, and outside community.

The arrangement couple tackles the same problem but uses intellectual reasoning for the self's wants and desires instead of using God's intended love. Ultimatums are usually given supporting others or something else over the mate, many times allowing a previous lifestyle or social network to compete with the mate. The only emotions surging are frustration from giving and taking, feelings of disrespect, and an awareness of not being loved. Usually, put-downs and negative gossip about the mate to family and friends result from this lack of love, and the cycle deepens until there is a break-up. Logically, they think that it is constructive criticism to put down the mate, but this is an error. Love never criticizes. *If it must correct, the WORD OF GOD will be used AS THE CORRECTOR between mates – NEVER A PERSON'S DISCIPLINE. We are to use the Word of God, the Bible, tenderly and lovingly (1 Cor. 13) to build up the mate, and communication between the two is beautiful, not strained or hurtful towards one another.* God's love is **NEVER** harsh, demeaning, slanderous, profane, inconsiderate, belittling – which is verbally abusive; **nor** *does it ever try* to physically control your mate by hitting, choking, or hurting them *in any way* – which is physically abusive. God's love is *never* **neglectful of it's protective duties;** it protects emotionally, physically, spiritually, financially, etc. **It never** withholds love from your mate in its verbal or body language *for any reason.* The *only* corrector and director for your mate should be the Word of God and the Holy Spirit. Never you. It is God (Jesus) who gives life to dead things (Rom 8:11, Rom 4:17) and God (the Holy Spirit) which brings revelation of this life, showing you your error (John 16:8); and He does so with such precision, that a person's life is never the same again (Heb. 4:12, 2 Cor. 5:17-18). Saul (before he was the apostle Paul) killed Christians (Acts 7:59). When Jesus changed his heart, the very thing that drove him to hurt others, now was driven by the Holy Spirit to love them so, he was not afraid of dying to show it and teach it (Acts 9, 2 Cor. 11:25). What he once killed for, he now will die for. That is a *complete* change. None of his old hurtful ways was in his new nature (2 Cor. 5:17). **This is the power of God.**The Lord is amazing.

> **"The cloud-nine emotions in a love affair melt a man and a woman together in the fire of a challenge and weld them into beautiful iron works of art.**
> **After the fire or challenge is gone, their relationship is even more beautiful than if they had not been through the fire."**
> Deborah L. Rivera

This is what God's love does. It is powerful, and God's love is always tested through the fire to see if it really is His.

What makes a love affair even more beautiful is that God *already has* the answers to situations and problems. The Word of God *is living* (Heb 4:12); it is not a man-made book of rules. The Word of God *is God Himself* (John 1:14) – He being the *almighty* power that is needed to bring change. His power is greater than any situation the world can bring. Satan has a certain amount of power to wreak havoc in people's lives; *but God's power is almighty*. There is no power greater or that can come close to it. Everything must obey His Word within His sovereignty. He's the creator. With this knowledge of God's power as their foundation, couples in a love affair just *love* through problems together in humility under the Word of God, resulting in a stronger love.

Because of satan and living in a fallen world, challenges will always be with us until we leave this earth, whether we are living a love affair or not. Jesus said in John 16:33 that "In the world ye shall have tribulation: but be of good cheer; I have overcome the world." Jesus said that His yoke is easy and His burdens are light (Matt. 11:30). I John 5:4 says, "For whatsoever is born of God overcometh the world: and this is the victory that overcometh the world, even our faith." Ephesians 5:23–28 tells husbands to love their wives as Christ loved the Church and gave Himself for it. Titus 2:4–5 and I Peter 3:1–6 tell wives to love and respect their husbands, even the ones who are not following the Word of God.

Just obeying these commandments eradicates a plethora of problems that may arise in challenges. *The Word of God is full of answers that **bring change** to life's dilemmas.*

God wants us to keep our prime focus on loving our mates while *He* takes the brunt of all trials, solving them through patience, faith, prayer, and confessing His Word. Sometimes, situations are solved immediately; sometimes, they are not. Regardless of either circumstance, He calls us to "wait" on Him in faith, not fear (Psalms 37, James 1:2-8).

"Wait on Him with a grateful heart in thankfulness and praising Him...loving your mate."
Louis L. Forté

Couples in arrangements are constantly trying to reinvent the wheel of problem solving because of selfishness. Their problem-solving methods seek to satisfy the selfish needs of themselves *rather than **trying to meet the needs of the other mate**, like love does.* Therefore, couples in arrangements are constantly *frustrated* in their lack of resolve, resulting in a strained relationship. ***Many grow tired of their partner under the false belief that they are incompatible, <u>not realizing that incompatibility is not the problem: they just don't have the love of God in them for their mates.</u>***

With solutions already worked out in the Word, it becomes important for couples to spend time together reading through the scriptures and praying together. As couples humbly do this, their individual habits begin to line up with God's blueprint, causing them to take on the habits and character of God. With this model of living, the love affair provides the opportunity for each mate to teach the other how to love him or her so that he or she can be the best in giving what the other needs the most.

This means that we are to give *all* situations to God and deal with them as He leads us in the fruit of the Spirit with our mate. This causes us to overlook the problem because it is in the Lord's hands now and keeps our focus on the love for our mates. It takes faith, which is one of the fruits of the Spirit. Faith in God's Word doesn't focus on the issue, but on His answers. It is a beautiful resolve. Placing cares on Jesus in faith takes the load and frustration away so that couples can continue living breezy, loving lives. **Now, it must be said that in certain situations that would endanger a life—such as cases of physical or sexual abuse—a person should not remain in a dangerous situation or endanger the lives of anyone else** such as their children, etc. God's love IS protection; *if we are not protecting, we are not loving.*

**"In a love affair,
when things go wrong,
couples stay loving toward each other."**
Louis L. Forté

Sometimes, when the Word of God is brought into a situation, a mate may refuse to comply with the Word out of stubbornness or a lack of understanding. In this instance, God calls for the couple to seek counsel. If counseling does not work, God says not to contend, argue, or give in to a sinful situation. We are not to give place to the devil (Eph. 4:27) but rather fast, pray, and forgive, having a meek and gentle spirit while pursuing peace, love, and holiness…never hesitating in still loving each other and putting each other first. ***Forgiveness in prayer keeps your love for the other mate alive!*** *The special feelings you have for your mate become encapsulated in* <u>*God's love of mercy,*</u> *which is the engine of forgiveness; and* **causes** *you to be patient, considerate, and loving towards your mate while waiting on God.* Again, it is God's love and faith in His promises that cause you to still have those special feelings toward your mate through trials while you wait.

When you start focusing on yourself, impatience sets in and causes those special feelings to die. **Patience resides only in God's love, forgiveness and His strength. Impatience resides in selfishness, un-forgiveness and our own strength**. The Bible says, "But let patience have her perfect work, that ye may be perfect and entire, wanting [lacking] nothing" (James 1:4). Let patience deal with this issue: Do not get in a rush. There is nothing impossible for him who believes; it takes faith. Jesus said, *"With men this is impossible; but with God all things are possible" (Matt. 19:26).* All God's promises are true. He takes the burden so that nothing and no one can separate you. He meant it when He said that the two shall become one. ***These special feelings are the instrument for holding this oneness through everything life can bring.*** That is why His love is so important to a relationship; **only** His love can sustain those special feelings each mate has for the other for a lifetime. God's utmost desire is "oneness" for a lifetime.

During any period of waiting, you must trust in His strength to carry the relationship until there is a breakthrough of His love and resolve in the situation. Sometimes during certain situations that have caused hurt or pain, or in seasons of standing against apathy, meanness or rudeness, it is easy for that specialness you hold dear for your mate to disappear momentarily. Hurt, anger, or neglect can blind you to the specialness of your love union with your mate. Or maybe, you sense a draining from a long wait period and feel completely like giving up. In whatever the situation, regardless of the presence of the special feelings God gave you for your mate, you are to always walk in love toward your mate as a rule, and let God take your love actions and turn them into loving feelings. You must forgive even before the guilty mate confesses his error and repents. Failure to forgive while in faith cancels God's declaration to answer your prayer. Jesus says in Mark 11:23-26,

> "For verily I say unto you, That whosoever shall say unto this mountain, Be thou removed, and be thou cast into the sea; and shall not doubt in his heart, but shall believe that those things which he sayeth shall come to pass; he shall have

63

whatsoever he saith. Therefore I say unto you, What things soever ye desire, when ye pray, believe that ye receive them, and ye shall have them. And when ye stand praying, forgive, if ye have ought against any: that your Father also which is in heaven may forgive you your trespasses. But if ye do not forgive, neither will your Father which is in heaven forgive your trespasses."

This is why we must not count our own lives as important but hold important what God wants for our love union with our mate and Him. It is loving Christ more that lets us die to ourselves and our own wants. It is easy for the flesh to seek its own way and give up because we do not feel love towards our mate during a period of our lives. To stand in faith, trust and forgiveness, really comes down to whether you love your flesh or Jesus more. If we say that we love Jesus more, our actions will prove it. The Bible says in Mark 8:34–35 that Jesus told His disciples, "Whoever desires to come after Me, *let him deny himself*, and *take up his cross*, and *follow Me. For whoever desires to save his life will lose it.*" It is the Holy Spirit who places a love in us for God greater than our own desires, and *changes* our desires to His desires.

The power of God to change a person's heart is *so real* and *powerfully amazing! He will amaze you!* He will *give you the strength to forgive* and cause the guilty mate *to see* his or her error, and *change them completely.* **He will** put His love into their hearts, and *change* their old ways to His new plan for their life. He is *the master* at this. He is the <u>only one</u> that can do this.

Romans 5:1–5 talks about how He gives us this love to believe Him during trials and tribulations we may face in life:

> "Therefore being justified by faith, we have peace with God through our Lord Jesus Christ: By whom also we have access by faith into this grace wherein we stand, and rejoice in hope of the glory of God. <u>And not only so, but</u> <u>we glory in tribulations also</u>: knowing that tribulation worketh patience; And patience, experience; and experience, hope: **And hope maketh not ashamed**; <u>**because the love of God is shed abroad in our hearts by the Holy Ghost which is given unto us.**</u>"

It is the job of the Holy Spirit to put the love of God in the situation that you are going through. There is nothing more powerful than God's love. It changes the heart of a man; therefore, outward actions become different. This is what is *needed* to have a love affair or change an arrangement into a love affair. Christ, through the power of the Holy Spirit, makes us conquerors in *all* that we encounter or face in life and in our marriages. The Apostle Paul said in Romans 8:35–39,

> "*Who shall separate us* from the love of Christ? Shall tribulation, or distress, or persecution, or famine, or nakedness, or peril, or sword? As it is written, For thy sake [Christ's sake] we are killed all the day long; we are accounted as sheep for the slaughter. Nay, **<u>in all these things we are more than conquerors</u> through him [Jesus Christ] that loved us.** For I am persuaded that neither death nor life, nor angels, nor principalities, nor powers, nor

things present, nor things to come, Nor height, nor depth, nor any other creature, shall be able to separate us from the love of God, which is in Christ Jesus our Lord."

At all times, we know Jesus Christ has given us **all** things to live life more abundantly. So by *faith* and *trust* in Him, through prayer, we have those things we are desiring and patiently waiting for. If it's 'love' you need from your husband, the promise is in Jesus. If it's 'love' you need from your wife, the promise is in Jesus. II Peter 1:3 says so wonderfully,

> "According as *his divine power* hath given unto us **all** *things* that pertain *unto life and godliness*, through the knowledge of him that hath called us to glory and virtue:"

Whatever is incomplete in your life, God sent Jesus to fulfill it. We are not to *look to* other humans, our mates, or to meet our needs. We are flawed and incapable. It is through the life-giving love of God in our mates, by the promises in Jesus, and the almighty power of the Holy Spirit to meet our needs in this world. He meets our needs through our mates when they are operating in Him. Only God is able to change the human heart (our mates) to flow in His love to meet that special need in our lives. Philippians 2:15 says, "For *it is God* which worketh in you both *to will* and *to do* of his good pleasure." God freely gives…all we have to do is receive.

"*I love* what God does to the human heart.
He is *the Master* of the human heart.
He is *truly* beautiful."
Deborah L. Rivera

While you are waiting and trusting in His promises, He keeps us in His perfect peace by telling us to keep our thoughts focused on what He has promised to give us. This is especially powerful during times of hardship in your relationship when you are prone to worry or are in a battle that needs much prayer, we are told in Philippians 4:6-8 and 2 Corinthian 10:3–5 to keep trusting:

> "**Be careful [anxious] for nothing**; but **in every thing** by prayer and supplication with thanksgiving let your requests be made known unto God. **And the peace of God**, which passeth all understanding, **shall keep your hearts and minds** through Christ Jesus. Finally, brethren, whatsoever things are true, whatsoever things are honest, whatsoever things are just, whatsoever things are pure, whatsoever things are lovely, whatsoever things are of good report; if there be any virtue, and if there be any praise, **think on these things**. Those things, which ye have both learned, and received, and heard, and seen in me, **do: and the God of peace shall be with you**."

> "For though we walk in the flesh [our humanity], **we do not war after the flesh**: **(For the weapons of our warfare are not carnal, but mighty through God to the pulling down of strongholds;) Casting**

**down imaginations, and every high thing that
exalteth itself against the knowledge of God, and
bringing into captivity every thought to the
obedience of Christ…**"

Knowing this…(1 John 5:4)

> "For whatsoever is born of God [all of His promises]
> *overcometh* the world: and this is the victory that
> *overcometh* the world, even our faith."

The weapons of our warfare that the Bible is referring to are
prayer, fasting (Matt. 17:21), walking in the Spirit (which is
walking in love and dying to the flesh), being faithful to God,
and trusting in Him above all.

It should be said that if we are dying to our flesh, we are *not*
doing those things we once did when we were in disobedience
or living a sinful lifestyle. This could be as simple as having a
mean or apathetic disposition towards your mate.

Living for Christ simply means that our lives are patterned after
Him. In 2 Corinthians 5:17–18, we are told, "Therefore if any
man be in Christ, he is a new creature: old things are passed
away; behold, all things are become new." And in 2 Corinthians
6:1, 3–10, this is confirmed again as we are told to live a
blameless ministry before Christ:

> "We then, as workers together with him (Jesus
> Christ), beseech you also that ye receive not the
> grace of God in vain. …**Giving no offence in any
> thing**, that the ministry be not blamed: But in all
> things approving ourselves as the ministers of God,

in much patience, in afflictions, in necessities, in distresses, In stripes, in imprisonments, in tumults, in labours, in watchings, in fastings; By pureness, by knowledge, by longsuffering, by kindness, by the Holy Ghost, by love unfeigned, By the word of truth, by the power of God, by the armour of righteousness on the right hand and on the left, By honour and dishonour, by evil report and good report: as deceivers, and yet true; As unknown, and yet well known, as dying and behold, we live; as chastened and not killed; As sorrowful, yet always rejoicing, and yet possessing all things."

For those who may be having difficulty with the way you talk to your mate, Colossians 4:6 says, "Let your speech be _always_ with grace, seasoned with _salt_ **[loving and gentle speech that will bless your mate, oppose sin and preserve from the corruption thereof—holy]**, that ye may know how ye ought to answer _every_ man."

To know that there is no situation greater than God, read I John 4:4: "Ye are of God, little children, and have overcome them: because greater is he [Jesus] that is in you, than he [Satan] that is in the world."

And lastly, we are told in Psalms 37:1-9,

> "Fret not thyself because of evildoers, neither be thou envious against the workers of iniquity. For they shall soon be cut down like the grass, and wither as the green herb. Trust in the Lord and do good; so shalt thou dwell in the land, and verily thou shalt be fed. Delight thyself also in the Lord:

and he shall give thee the desires of thine heart. Commit thy way unto the Lord; trust also in him; and he shall bring it to pass. And he shall bring forth thy righteousness as the light, and thy judgment as the noonday. Rest in the Lord, and wait patiently: fret not thyself because of him who prospereth in his way, because of the man who bringeth wicked devices to pass. Cease from anger, and forsake wrath: fret not thyself in any wise to do evil. For evildoers shall be cut off: but those that wait upon the Lord, they shall inherit the earth."

Again, God gives a plethora of answers for marital or relationship success in oneness, as well as life. Anything evil in a relationship or in the home, does not have the authority or power over God to stay. We must be careful when saying that a person or situation cannot change. If this statement was true, then the purpose of our Lord's death was in vain, and He does not hold all authority and power over satan. But as we know, this is not true (Luke 10:19, 1 John 4:4). With man it is impossible, but with God, ALL things are possible. Trusting God has been the main problem for mankind from Genesis to Revelation. God gives a reference "not to fear" for every day of the year. We must trust Him and what He says for our lives.

"And now abideth faith, hope, charity, these three; but the greatest of these is _charity [love]_."
I Corinthians 13:13

Walking in the Spirit at all times with your mate is paramount, whether there is a challenge or not. Walking in the fruit of the

Spirit has powerful influences on our mates. It is not just what we say but **how** we say it to them—*our attitude or unspoken language* as well as what we do or do not do for them. If you want to gauge how your mate might be considering you, *look at how you treat them*. The Bible says that we will recognize people by their fruits (Matt. 7:16–20). They are weighing you by your fruit. Does your fruit in how you treat your mate resemble God? Does it produce a love affair?

> **"Your mate is the most valuable entity in the world. Anything that is of value demands to be treated with respect."**
> Louis L. Forté

The fruit of the Spirit is the kind of love we must give to our spouses when putting them first. When this love has its way in our relationships, life is lived to its fullest.

The Lord, who created a love affair, has all the answers for any concern a relationship may experience. This is why God calls us to crucify our flesh daily, being holy, not being lukewarm, and living from the supernatural side of life. His commands have strong implications on our marriages.

> **"Be ye holy, as I am holy."**
> I Peter 1:16

Holding Important What God Holds Important: Godly character in loving your mate when dealing with sin and situations surrounding your relationship

Our bodies are the most precious, valuable, and irreplaceable gifts from God; our bodies do not belong to us. Our body is the temple where God dwells. "Know ye not that your body is the temple of the Holy Ghost which is in you, which ye have of God, and ye are not your own? For ye are bought with a price: therefore glorify God in your body, and in your spirit, which are God's" (I Cor. 6:19, 20). We cannot do anything we want with our bodies; similarly, we cannot do anything we want with our life—both belong to God. We cannot talk any kind of way, watch any kind of thing, participate in any kind of action, or dress any kind of way. The King lives within us. Our lives and lifestyles must represent kingdom living. What we do with our bodies and our lives must align with His Word.

The Bible was given for doctrine, reproof, correction, and instruction in righteousness (II Tim. 3:16). The Bible says of wrongful situations or sin left unchecked, "Your glorying is not good. Know ye not that a little leaven leaveneth the whole lump?" (I Cor. 5:6). We are called to be the salt of the earth (Matt. 5:13). The Bible is clear that we are not supposed to leave sin ignored. Salt stings a little when poured into a wound, but it is good for the wound. It stops the wound from rotting; it heals the wound. This is good. The same effect occurs with the Word of God. Godly correction, when poured into a sinful or wrong situation, stops Satan from increasing the corruption and gaining a stronger foothold in the relationship. Notice the escalation of Satan's ways: pride turns into insensitivity, apathy, death to intimacy, or emotional death. Control turns into belittling, meanness, devious behavior, abuse, and then physical death.

"Ingratitude leads to blindness and being dull of hearing towards the blessings one's mate brings; this leads to harsh treatment and indifference towards these blessings,
ultimately destroying **the special feelings of love these mates once had."**
Louis L. Forté

Flirting turns into ungodly/unhealthy relationships, to adultery, then to divorce. <u>Satan never stops at discomfort</u>. His only mission is to steal, kill, and destroy (John 10:10). He does not stop until the relationship or you are destroyed. This is why the scriptures also tell us in Ephesians 4:26 to **give no place** to the devil and in Proverbs 22:3 that a prudent man **<u>foresees</u>** evil and **<u>hides</u>** himself, but a foolish man *goes on and is punished.*

When Satan is present in a relationship, the evidence in obvious. There is a lack of contentment, misunderstanding, sinful behavior, covenant-breaking behavior with those of the opposite sex, adulterous affairs (whether physical or emotional by ungodly soul ties), addictions, unhealthy behavioral attachments within family, within friendships or towards work or extracurricular activities; there is meanness, rudeness, insensitivity, belittling, unfaithfulness, ego, pride, apathy or indifference, stubbornness, laziness, insensible faultfinding or nitpicking, and the list goes on.

The sinful nature of our flesh (Jam. 1:13–15) and the influence of Satan and his demons are always the causes of hurtful, ungodly actions to the relationship. Nothing demons do produces a beautiful end. *Nothing in our sinful nature is love.* This is why we can't put our trust in the fallen nature of mankind. **To tell someone you have to trust your mate just for the sake of trusting them is inaccurate**. You can *only trust* the genuine *love of God* in people's lives; the love which brings about His holiness, His character, His faithfulness, and His honesty in their lives, *which they are an example of*, not their "say-so" love only – because all "stated-love" from mankind is faulty. It is foolishness to put your trust in the fallen nature of man, *knowing* God's love is absent or in the background of their lives. **Trust is born of God, not of man. This is why many seemingly good people have committed adultery, or have been caught doing something that has shocked the majority of those that knew them. These people were shocked because they put the kind of trust in them that they could never do that kind of wrong, but this is where the mistake was made…we can *only* put our trust in God's love; _only_ He is perfect and can't do any wrong**. His love brings life; never death. The *best* of mankind was born into sin, so to say, "Oh he/she would never do that," is foolish. *This is why God gives us HIS WISDOM and HIS LOVE and HIS HOLINESS to guide our steps.* Doing anything on our own…we will error. We need to follow God in everything we do.

"Without *God's love* and *His wisdom* in a relationship, you can't have trust…Trust belongs to Him, it doesn't belong to man."
Deborah Rivera

Satan focuses upon destroying a marriage or a future marriage more than any other relationship because God places the most importance on the relationship between a man and his woman. Therefore, Satan's ways neglect the importance of walking in God's character in a couple's relationship. <u>God's character always puts the needs of your mate first</u>. It always first protects the position, care, and integrity of your mate. Satan causes people to neglect the first priority of their mate. He deceives them to choose the needs of others over their mate, or he deceives them to allow the wrongs of others to exist without challenge.

Many times in relationships, ingratitude keeps mates from hearing the truth from one another. Ingratitude is a sin with extreme destructive results because it blinds your eyes and makes you dull of hearing *to the truth*. This happens especially when wives try to tell their husbands something which is true, builds their covenant, gives instruction to apply Godly wisdom or admonishes a Godly lifestyle; the husband knows that she is right, but out of ingratitude, pride, and a lack of God's love, he will silence her or be reluctant to do it. This is ingratitude, not being grateful for the distinctive function that God has given you in the female gender of yourself (and same for the husband to the wife).

When husbands or wives listen to other people, including their children, instead of their mates, that's not only being ungrateful, but, even viler, *it is an act of treachery* that <u>breaks trust</u> in the covenant they have with each other and God. Putting others first destroys oneness. It is quite amazing how husbands and wives will choose to put others over their mates, and usually these other people do not live with, take care of, or provide support for them. It is your mate who serves and meets your needs, but when your mate tries to tell you something *which God would honor*, you do not even consider it. You ignore her or him and do what you want to do, or take someone else's word over your mate's. Regardless of the situation, you are not to take someone else's word over your mate's. This is vile to God. When God said that He would make man a helpmate (Gen. 2:18), it was because man needed help. Adam and Eve needed the help from each other, just like all in the Trinity need help from each other. You can receive help only from someone who knows something you do not, or functions in a capacity that you do not. Whether you are a husband or wife, your mate has something that you need. God does not like when we do not value our mates; that is why He gave them to us. When you try to operate solo, without consulting your mate, you are operating on half of the ability when you are supposed to be operating in oneness, not a half. Remember, you are only a half a person in marriage; your mate brings the other half. The two shall become one. One + one = one.

Now, you could argue with God, but again, you cannot outlive God to prove God wrong. After death, you are totally at His mercy. All of _your rules_ that you lived by here on earth _will change to His law_. Time is on God's side. He is time. He is eternity. He is yesterday. He is today, tomorrow, and forever. No man can find Him out, lest He reveal Himself to him, which He has done through His Word, Jesus Christ, and the Holy Spirit. Every man will stand in the judgment; every knee will bow, and every tongue will confess that Jesus Christ is Lord. Earthly living was designed by God for mankind. Here, we can make choices freely. We can believe what Jesus said in His Word or reject it. It is wise to consider that before any human was created, Jesus was already here and will be here when we die. This is humbling and requires sincere consideration. Time will cease after death. Time will be no more. There are only two destinations, heaven or hell. Every word that Jesus spoke is spirit and life. Our words and our actions have a destination; they are carrying us to their destination, heaven or hell. Whether we believe and live in agreement with God or live outside His will, there is a destination.

"If what you believe can't defend you before God, why believe it?"
Louis L. Forté

God created husbands and wives to live in His image, the love union of the Trinity. This means that **_we were created to love_ because God is love**. Therefore, it is impossible to try to live outside of the *love* He created us for. Think for a moment: say that we were designed to be a thoroughbred horse intended to race but *we refuse* to be that. Instead, *we choose* to live like a mule. There is no way that a mule mentality will keep a thoroughbred happy, fulfilled, etc. If we want to be fulfilled in this earth's realm, we must be and live out what God created us to be in our marriages. Just as Jesus is the door to all of life, your wife or husband is the door to physical life. God did not create us just to exist. You can have spiritual life here on earth without marriage, die, and go to heaven. But physical life is quite different; its only need is here in the earth. The best of physical life is in marriage…God's love affair.

"People who won't change when they are wrong have the most problems in life."
Louis L. Forté

John Bevere, a minister and the best-selling author of *Breaking Intimidation*, spoke of sin and how we treat it: either by false humility or with Godly character. He said of sin,

"A person is seduced into sin when he counts as common or familiar what God esteems as holy. Too often, we take lightly the things God takes seriously, and we treat seriously the things God treats lightly. *We are very serious about appearing respectable to other people* [emphasis added], but that is not as important to God as the motives of our hearts. I have known men who were entrapped in sin, all the while saying, 'I love Jesus.' They measured their spiritual condition by what they felt for Jesus. But did they love Him enough to die to that sin that bound them? No, they had no fear of God!" [3]

Bevere also spoke of people who see sin or wrong in situations but do nothing, thinking that it is not their position to correct a situation in fear of judging others, being too harsh, etc. He said that God calls this the "fear of man" and/or false humility: these people neglect pursuing God's character. Rather, we are told not to neglect the gift of God in pursing God's character by giving us the example of Paul's letter to Timothy, in which Bevere says:

"[In 1 Tim 4:14] Paul stressed to Timothy the importance of not neglecting the gift of God…To elaborate on what it means not to neglect the gift, let's look at some antonyms. The opposite of neglect is to: Accomplish, achieve, act, attend, care for, complete, conclude, consider, consummate. All of these words are words of *action* and *authority*….They are positive and decisive…. To neglect [is to] breach, disdain, dismiss, disregard, discount, ignore, underestimate, overlook, undervalue,

[3] From *Breaking Intimidation* (p. 136), by John Bevere, 1995, 2006, Lake Mary, Florida: Charisma House, AStrang Company. Copyright 1995, 2006. Reprinted with permission.

scorn, and despise. These are all negative words *signifying a lack of action, decisiveness, and authority.* It is a serious and weighty thing to neglect what is entrusted to us. We suffer loss when we neglect.... [He says of people living in false humility that] people living in such a state recognize the importance of pursuing God's character but stop there. They never venture out into God's gifting in their lives because they are afraid. They avoid anything that involves confrontation, perceiving it as a lack of love or Christian character. I refer to these people as 'peacekeepers.' At first glance, peacekeeping may look appealing, but Jesus never said, 'Blessed are the peacekeepers.' Rather, He said, 'Blessed are the peacemakers, for they shall be called sons of God' (Matt. 5:9). A peacekeeper avoids confrontation at any cost. He will go to any length to preserve a false sense of security for himself, which he mistakes for peace.

A peacemaker, on the other hand, will boldly confront no matter what it may cost him because he does not worry about himself. Instead, he is motivated by his love for God and truth. Only under these conditions can true peace thrive. There is peace in the kingdom of God (Rom. 14:17). However, this peace does not come by the absence of confrontation. As Jesus pointed out, 'The kingdom of heaven suffers violence, and the violent take it by force' (Matt. 11:12). There is violent opposition to the advancement of God's kingdom. Often we think, I'll just ignore this, and it will go away. But we need to wake up and realize that what we do not confront will not change! This is why Jude urges on the saints with the following: 'Beloved, while I was very diligent to write to you concerning our common salvation, I found it necessary to write to you exhorting you to contend earnestly for the faith which was once for all delivered to the saints' (Jude 3). Notice he said 'contend earnestly,' not hope for the best. Contend means to fight or wage battle. Christianity is not an easy lifestyle! There is constant opposition and resistance to our pursuit of God in both the natural and the spiritual realms! Paul strengthened Timothy with, 'You therefore must endure hardship as a good soldier of Jesus Christ. *No one engaged in warfare entangles himself with the affairs of this life; that he may please him (God) who hath chosen him to be a soldier. And if a man also strive for masteries, yet is he not crowned, except he strive lawfully'* (II Tim. 2:4, 5) [emphasis added].We are engaged in warfare. *We are to have the attitude of a soldier* [emphasis added]. We are not to back down from evil, but overcome it with good (Rom. 12:21)."[4]

Regarding our roles in *oneness*, when you neglect putting your mate first, you may recognize the importance of pursuing God's character *as a mate* **for your covenant**, but you stop there.

You neglect _God's purpose_ for the attributes He gave you as the male person or female person of your covenant. *Situations that call for your attributes to take on their Godly purpose* **you avoid**. For example, flirting is designed to pull one into a bond between two people, whether emotional, physical, temporary, or lasting. God created the purpose of flirting to attract and keep your mate, not to destroy the bond between mates. So when a male or female mate flirts outside of their covenant, or *allows* the opposite sex outside their covenant to flirt with them, he or

---

[4] John Bevere, Breaking *Intimidation* (p. 26-28), Reprinted with permission.

she is lending his or her God-given attributes for the covenant to the works of darkness; this is Satanic, and God takes it seriously. **Anything that *works against* what God is trying to build is from the Evil One.**

"Outside flirting is *covenant-breaking behavior* that *pulls you* out of your covenant with your mate and God.
Anything
That works in the opposite direction of God's commands or works against His covenant follows after sin...it is destroying what He is trying to build."
Deborah L. Rivera

Being attracted to others outside of your marriage or relationship pulls your heart away from your Godly attribute to protect your covenant with your mate and God. It also destroys that protective covering of what is special only between you and your mate. It adulterates it because this covenant is holy. It is spiritual. **This covenant *is God's bond, not ours*.** God designed flirting to attract then maintain the bonds of two people who have *entered into a promise or covenant*, whether implied or stated. Whether you are married or just in a relationship, flirting should ***only*** come from, and be shared within, that relationship; *any outside flirting is not from God and absent of God's presence*. Your attractions should only be for your mate.

Many people dismiss outside flirting while in a relationship as harmless and normal, but God holds important for us to *esteem our attributes for our mates as holy*, to protect *what **He** is* *forming* between you and your mate. <u>Even with "just looking"</u> <u>to admire someone outside of your covenant, *it is love* – God's</u> <u>beautiful love that causes you *to reserve that action **only** for*</u> *your mate*. We were created to honor God, not serve ourselves. God's love won't cause you to go outside for anything; you have all that you need with your mate. Straying follows looking. *Looking lures you away:* **God never lures you** out of His covenant; selfishness does. You look on purpose to please yourself; not God, nor your mate. Again, we need to walk in His wisdom…His love. *It takes more to live in this kind of pure love, than anything else professed by man.*

Bevere accurately states, "In their [people's] pursuit to be balanced, normal and accepted, they have forgotten God does not call 'normal' what the world calls 'normal.' When you truly love God and fear Him alone, you will live a life of consecration, not worldliness."[5]

Satan thrives on using outside distractions to ensnare people. By creating desire of any kind outside your relationship, *it distracts you away from your mate*. Whatever lusteth *against* the will of the Spirit [the Holy Spirit] is sin; *this doesn't have to be just sexual.* Galatians 5:16–17 says, "This I say then, Walk in the Spirit, and ye shall not fulfil the lust of the flesh. For the flesh ***lusteth against the Spirit,*** and the Spirit *against* the flesh: and these are contrary the one to the other: so that ye can not do the things that ye would."

When we make common this adulterous kind of emotional or physical sin, it destroys the *trust* or oneness between mates which is of God. This kind of behavior tears apart the love union God created to mimic the Trinity's. This is why God

---

[5] John Bevere, Breaking Intimidation, p.130

takes it so seriously; ***He calls it treachery against your mate***, and ***He hates it***. Jesus said in Matthew 5:28 that to even look at another woman and lust in your heart after her is to commit adultery. This means all you have to do is "look" at another person with desire other than your mate and you have committed adultery. God's Word goes further to say in James 1:13–15 that **any temptation**, again, *not just sexual*, that pulls you out of God's will is evil. Why? *All temptation* comes from the Evil One; God cannot tempt anyone:

> "Let no man say when he is temped, I am tempted of God: for God cannot be tempted with evil, neither tempteth he any man: But when he is tempted, when he is ***drawn away*** of his ***own lust*** and enticed. Then when lust hath conceived, it bringeth forth sin: and sin, when it is finished, bringeth forth death."

Thereby, being attracted by someone's friendliness, their intellect, their likeability, and other seemingly innocent gestures can be held as sin against you *when you allow these things to draw you away from* your covenant with your mate. The emotion in your heart may not start as something sexual, but likewise, *it draws you away* from your mate. This is how emotional adultery starts. It usually starts as something casual, not sexual. But anything of Satan is never meant as harmless. Just as James 1:13-15 explains, all temptations lead to death to whatever God is trying to do. Let us also not forget Proverbs 14:12, "There is a way which seemeth right unto a man, but the end thereof are the ways of death." All outside people should use their attributes to respect God's covenant you have with your mate; not to challenge or weaken it through any action that disregards, disrespects, or ***tries to share a place*** in your covenant.

It is God's will for us to use our attributes, and all that is within us, to honor the covenant with our mate. When a man or a woman is **not** *using his or her attributes for God's purpose in their covenant*, the other mate *senses it right away*, **and trust is broken**. Man is a spirit. TRUST IS SPIRITUAL. TRUST IS GOD. When the devil touches this trust, it is known right away in your inner spirit. **God sees** *this broken trust forming in your heart; this hurts Him, because not only is He a part of this covenant, but He sees you and your mate as one. You are hurting and destroying the trust of "your self." That is why He* hates *outside flirting.* **He watches, hurt,** *as His covenant begins to break.*

A break-up of trust or oneness *starts long before it is expressed externally*. This, as mentioned above, is one of Satan's steps to death. This is why it is so important to hold important what God holds important—to put the protection of your mate's position in your covenant of high importance. He takes His created covenant for relationships seriously. He takes His creation for a love affair seriously. Third parties have no place in our hearts.

Flirting and emotional adultery weakens or breaks *His* covenant: it breaks trust. This is why *God wants us vigilant and watchful*, ready to hate this unholy behavior as He does. It is evil to use our attributes to *work towards destroying* what God has designed to join together. God says in Proverbs 8:13 that the fear of the Lord is to **hate evil**. *When you do not hate what God hates*, and you accept flirting or emotional attachments outside your marriage, *you despise God*; otherwise, you would hold *His* relationship, *His* covenant important.
When you accept this unholy behavior as normal, you dismiss the problems that arise in your marriage or relationship because

of your pride and your love for the world; these unholy characteristics cause you to take a 'peacekeeping' attitude[6]. You allow this outside person to steal the God-given rights from your mate and from the covenant because you fear losing this demonic attention that boosts your lusts, ego or your pride. Therefore, selfishness causes *you to avoid extinguishing* this kind of adulterous behavior; instead, you rationalize that it is not that serious. This causes you to take a lack of concern in confronting it. Your allegiance is now divided between God and the devil. Jesus said in Mark 3:25 that a house divided against itself cannot stand. ***Pride, ego, and selfishness cause you to rationalize against confronting it.*** The flesh causes you to place more importance on maintaining this demonic source that is feeding your pride and covetousness even though the outside person is destroying your covenant with your mate and God. Keeping the peace with these injurious parties takes precedence rather than making the situation right for your marriage or relationship. This process of rationalizing *is deadly* for a covenant as it begins to *twist* what God hates into something that is OK to do. Pride does this, just like it did to Lucifer. As you begin to believe that it is OK to flirt, or that flirting is not that serious, you can become so deceived that you turn on your mate, accusing them of a jealous spirit, *which is in error*. You cannot be jealous of yourself or jealous of your own covenant – it's already 'yours.' You can, and are supposed to, be protective over the covenant, which causes you *to notice and express your noticing* of the breach. Jealousy, covetousness, and envy mainly come *from the outside party*; they want what you have in the covenant with your mate. It should be mentioned that not only is the injured mate noticing your sin; ***God is noticing and***

---

[6] John Bevere, *Breaking Intimidation*, p. 27

feeling the same way your mate is feeling. He is a part of your love union.

When pride and lack of love in the guilty mate cause him to twist "protectiveness" into "jealousy," this ploy takes the focus off the guilty mate's sin and perpetrates it on the innocence and protectiveness of the injured mate. This is vile. Nothing could be further from the truth. Satan always distorts the truth *so that the focus will not be on him*; he thus will be able to stay and penetrate more. Emotional adultery is a break of trust or covenant; it is a precursor to physical adultery. And if further unchecked, pride can cloud one's vision so much that the guilty mate won't even detect or notice his/her own sin or the sin of the outside party. Psalm 36:1–4 says,

> "The transgression of the wicked saith within my heart, that there is no fear of God before his eyes. For he *flattereth himself* [emphasis added] in his own eyes, until his iniquity be found to be hateful. The words of his mouth are iniquity and deceit: *he hath left off to be wise, and to do good* [emphasis added]. He deviseth mischief upon his bed; he setteth himself in a way that is not good; he abhorreth not evil."

It is never in the act of God's wisdom, nor His goodness *for you* to be drawn away from your mate, or allow others to *disrespect, share or steal your mate's position* within the covenant. All covenant-breaking behavior is death to the covenant between your mate, you, and God. God says that we are to act in a sincere way, not to break the trust of our mates, emotionally or physically, or else our prayers will not be heard. In the case of physical adultery, it says in Malachi 2:13–16 (NKJV),

86

"...You cover the altar of the Lord with tears, with weeping and crying; so He [God] does not regard the offering anymore, nor receive it with goodwill from your hands. Yet you say, 'For what reason' Because the Lord has been witness between you and the wife of your youth, with whom you have dealt treacherously; Yet she is your companion and your wife by covenant. But did He [God] not make them one, having a remnant of the Spirit? And why one? He seeks godly offspring [sin against your mate affects generations]. Therefore take heed to your spirit, and let none deal treacherously with the wife of his youth. For the Lord God of Israel says that He hates divorce, for it covers one's garment [one's wife] with violence, says the Lord of hosts. Therefore take heed to your spirit, that you do not deal treacherously."

Trust is the binding factor of a promise or a covenant. It is *God's* glue within *His bond*. Without it, <u>you have nothing</u>. When God says that He hates divorce, He means any divorce pertaining to the covenant. This means emotional divorce from an emotional lack of trust, or a physical divorce from a physical act that breaks trust. This is why we are not to allow flirting or any other covenant-breaking behavior to exist when we are in a relationship, <u>no matter how subtle</u>. *No secret attractions of any kind, for any another person, fantasy or real, should exist in our hearts. God sees.* God says in Matthew 19:6, "Wherefore they are no more twain [two], but one flesh. What God hath joined together, let not man put asunder [separate]." You are not to let anyone in the slightest cause your mate to wonder; that would be causing her or his trust to deteriorate or break. <u>You are not to dismiss flirting as being ok, or dismiss having emotional attachments with people outside your covenant as</u>

being ok when you are married or in a relationship; regardless of who they are and your past relationship with them. *This kind of behavior works against God.* **Your mate takes precedence**. We have a standard to uphold.

The love covenant must permeate every facet of your relationship, keeping all intruders out. Outside flirting could never be apart of either spouse's life when they love God more than themselves or anyone else, and if they are loving each other more than their selves or anyone else. This is the foundation on which God's love affair between a husband and wife is built. Now, with that said, the only thing husbands and wives should not give each other is worship. Both husband and wife should love God more than themselves. *Worship belongs to God alone.* As for the relationship, couples should love each other so passionately that nothing earthly should draw them away from their covenant, but all worship belongs to God.

> **"Dear Lord, work in me to will and do your good pleasure; and let my will be lost in thine. Give me victory over my greatest enemy; Give my victory over my self-will... and let my will be lost in thine. Amen."**
> Prayer by Louis L. Forté of Phil. 2:13

As it was said earlier, God does not want us to be peacekeepers, allowing wrongdoing and unholy situations to prevail. As John Bevere reveals, we are told by Christ to be peacemakers[7] or *to do something* to *bring God's truth into a situation; to uphold God's character surrounding our relationships*. God loves

---

[7] John Bevere, *Breaking Intimidation*, p. 27

peacemakers: ***they boldly confront*** *who or whatever the situation is, no matter what it costs them.* <u>They do this with no hesitation because they are not doing it for themselves. Instead, they are motivated by their love for God and for their mate.</u> **It is a serious thing to neglect what is entrusted to us by the Lord.** The Lord has entrusted us to put our mates first, *cherishing and protecting their trust* and surrounding our relationships with holiness. He places high importance on protecting those special feelings that give priority, foster trust, and maintain oneness in a relationship. *We suffer loss whenever we neglect His commands or gifts.* To have a love affair, you ***must*** be a peacemaker of the Lord for your mate…for *your* self.

The Lord's way has some resistance to it; it makes you strong, stable, and humble on the inside, considerate and loving towards your mate, and with a finish that is wonderful…true love. With kindness and wisdom, we are to humbly correct our mates and others when they are wrong, considering our own selves as if we were tempted in the same situation that they are (Gal. 6:1). We would want them to love us enough to not let us or our relationship self-destruct but rather tell us the truth in love. This is the Bible's way. Galatians 5:1 says, "Stand fast in the liberty wherewith Christ has made us free, and be not entangled again with the yoke of bondage." We are to stand in peace, stand in love, stand in kindness.

> **"Where Christ is, <u>there is freedom</u>. Where freedom is, there is <u>holiness</u>. Any kind of sin is bondage."**
> Louis L. Forté

Jesus sent us the Holy Spirit to help us (John 16:7) live free from sin. The Holy Spirit is the one who puts God's love into our hearts and causes us to act out this love between each other in our relationship with our mate. Without Him, our flesh will not be strong enough or able to attain the <u>love of God</u> for the patience and tenderness needed to protect these most important loving feelings. That is why we are told to guard our hearts with all diligence, for out of it are the issues of life (Prov. 4:23). We are to guard the presence of the Holy Spirit in our love towards our mate. He is the giver of strength. He is the giver of love. He is the giver of kindness and tenderness. *He is the giver of those very special feelings.* <u>Without Him, we are nothing</u>.

Sin is a horrible thing to participate in. Scripture says in Numbers 32:23 that our sins will find us out. When we practice sin, we are doing wrong without repentance. We live on in iniquity, which is sowing to our flesh. Scripture says that sowing to the flesh reaps corruption; when sin has finished, it brings death (Gal. 6:8 and James1:15). This was shown earlier—how Satan's ultimate end spiritually, emotionally, and physically for a relationship is death. All of Satan's stuff in your heart or all of his ways in your life lead to death.

Hebrews 12:11 says, "Now no chastening for the present seemeth to be joyous, but grievous: nevertheless *afterward* it yielded the *peaceable fruit of righteousness* **unto them** <u>which are exercised thereby</u>." Though the initial confrontation of speaking God's truth may be slightly uncomfortable, the end results are beautiful. When any wrong turns to right, the result is true peace. This is God's government for living, living in His peace, which is beyond anything the world can give.

This is why God demands holiness. This is *His* first love. Not letting God's love deal with problems opens the door for more of the devil's influence in the marriage. For the time being, his influence seems quiet, but this is temporary. The true problem has not been eliminated but simmers just beneath the surface. Every time it surfaces, it grows stronger. Love emotions die little by little. This is the devil's method of deception. As the situation lingers, frustration sets in and turns to anger, then to bitterness, which can result in vile, vengeful behavior, whether stealthily or boldly.

This is why to have a love affair a couple must be born again; we cannot combat flesh or sin without it.

To have a love affair, a couple must be born again

"You can't cope with life
if you don't have the gift of life (Jesus)."
Louis L. Forté

In Genesis 1:26–27, God said to Jesus and the Holy Spirit, "Let us make man in our image, after our likeness and let them have dominion over the fish of the sea, and over the fowl of the air, and over the cattle, and over all the earth and over every creeping thing that creepeth upon the earth. … So God created man in His own image. In the same image of God, created He him, male and female, He created them."

As we covered earlier, when God made Adam (and Eve) in the Garden of Eden, He blew the breath of life into him, and he became a living being. What God blew into him was Himself.

"Since God is a spirit, He could only blow His spirit into Adam. Therefore, Adam became not just a living being but a *spiritual* being created *in the likeness of God—love—God is love.*"
Louis L. Forté

But when Adam and Eve chose to follow Satan and sinned, sin separated them from God's love, and they took on the nature of Satan. The beautiful love affair God had gifted to Adam and Eve turned into dominion and servant hood: a war affair. But God had a plan to restore His original design for a love affair through the shed blood of Jesus for our sins. Because of God's great love and compassion, seeing our inability to come to Him, He came to us.

"For God so loved the world that He gave His only begotten Son that whosoever believeth in Him should not perish but have everlasting life."
John 3:16

This is why it is impossible for us to change our wrongful ways or any Satanic ideas that were planted in us as children. Our flesh embraces what is wrong; it is comfortable in the presence of wrong. Only Christ stirs us inside and makes it impossible for us to be comfortable with sin. It is imperative that we surrender to a new life in the Holy Spirit. Even if someone grew up watching his parents in a great arrangement, anything less than God is of the flesh and not of Him. Couples will need to submit to the leading of the Holy Spirit in changing their lives to God's love affair. It must start on the inside before an outward transformation is seen.

God saw that mankind without Him was lost in Satan's ways, full of selfishness, self-will, self-righteousness, and pride, without hope and void of all righteousness. God sent Jesus as the final sacrifice to die for our sins (John 3:16). To love us, Jesus had to die because life is in the blood and the wages of sin was death. Our sin brought us death. Our just due was hell. Jesus came and died on our behalf so that we could escape death and hell. Not only that; Jesus came that we might have life, and have life more abundantly (John 10:10). So, He came not only to save us from hell but to enable us to live free from our past sinful natures that Satan ruled. This is why those who do not have Christ as their Lord or those who have an erroneous view of scripture do not have the help of the Holy Spirit, who is the only one able to help us live in God's true love with our mates. Without a correct understanding of God's love, His ways, and His commandments, there can never be a love affair.

If Jesus died for love, if He died for His bride (the Church), we are to follow His example and die daily for our mate. Self must die; our flesh must die that Christ may live in and through us. Dying is experienced when we choose to bring holiness and the love of oneness first and foremost to our mates when our flesh would rather do something different. It is easy to be selfish, to hold secret attractions of people other than your mate, or act in a way towards your mate *where you just do not care*. It will take dying to situations like these; for example, simply caring about *all* the things that matter to your mate, or by protecting your mate from outside flirting even when they are not present. Dying to the flesh is choosing to live like Christ. It costs your doing your own thing when Christ tells you to do something different. **It is not playing the role; it is being the genuine article:** *a real love affair in the Lord*.

93

"You only keep in life what you are <u>excited</u> about. *Make it a love affair* that you are excited about."
Louis L. Forté

It is unfortunate to note, but there are many people also who proclaim that they are living for Christ, but the weapons of mass destruction are still hurtfully evident in their actions and their relationships or mattiages. God and Satan cannot exist in the same action. These people unfortunately are not rightly dividing the Word of God (II Tim. 2:15), and what He really means for us to live humbly in His love, holiness, and wisdom with our mates. Without the Holy Spirit to teach us, we can tragically fall into error, misjudging and misguiding our actions with what the scripture is truly saying. We need a correct understanding of God's love *for our mates* to fulfill His will in our marriages. Bevere also states,

> "We have become experts in His [God's] goodness; however, it is not just His goodness we are to consider. We must understand the severity of God as well. His goodness draws us to His heart, and His severity keeps us from pride and all manner of sin. A person who only considers the goodness [of God] forsakes the fear that will keep him from pride and worldliness. Likewise, the person who only considers the severity of God is easily ensnared in legalism. It is both the love and the fear of God that keep us on the narrow path to life."[8]

We must remember, God's love embodies the totality of God…He does not tell us to love our neighbor any way we

---

[8] John Bevere, *Breaking Intimidation*, p. 135

please. *He is a consuming fire against **all** that works against His Word* (Heb 12:28)*: this is the fear of God.* When we yield our entire lives to God, to love Him with all our hearts, not to pick and choose from Him to fit our lifestyles; the Holy Spirit will put the totality of God's love – His wisdom, the fear of God, and His life-building love – into our hearts...*causing us **to hate what He hates** and **love what He loves***. God is love, but He is also a consuming fire (1 Jn 4:8, Heb 12:28)...we can't separate Him to fit our own agenda.

To the dating or engaged:
So why is the love covenant for a love affair important to you?

The tragedy of not understanding God's true design for marriage is that most couples prove out these special feelings by getting married without fully understanding that these special emotions are supposed to easily remain and grow by God's love of oneness. Most couples are taught that these emotions will change for the worse and that it will be an uphill battle to keep them. So, they take vows, for better or worse, through sickness and health, *waiting* for the feelings to die and *accepting it* when they do encounter challenges or differences. **They are taught to prepare for an arrangement, so they immediately structure their lives for one even before they say "I do"** instead of preparing their lives to continue their ecstasy in a love affair with each other and Jesus Christ. As the marriage relationship is to mirror the relationship of Jesus and the Church, prior to marriage, we are supposed to see our future marriage growing in Jesus Christ and loving each other more and more (Eph. 5). Once the "idea" is taught or implanted that two people have to work so hard at marriage, many end up in a war affair.

Therefore, in the premarital stage, it is of utmost importance that couples are taught God's design for a love affair. Once this idea is received in their hearts and becomes a part of them, they will naturally begin living out a love affair and will do so even before marriage.

"WHY" is a little word that gives much insight into the reasons why couples choose one another and why these feelings last as long as they do after marriage. This self-counsel using WHY should be used by all couples. This will immediately reveal whether your mate or future mate of choice has God's design for a love affair in him or her. If he or she is not exemplifying God's love for a love affair, you are experiencing the weapons of mass destruction.

When couples do not use the question "WHY am I with this person?" as a lever to evaluate the mate in comparison to God's love affair, most of the time they end up "marrying a stranger" with weapons of mass destruction in tow. Only God's design for a love affair allows you the closeness to get to know your mate beyond the confines of normal friendship. God steps in and binds you with a knowing of each other that goes beyond the physical. You become one. Arrangements always result in a limited friendship of two separate people enjoying brief moments of mediocre intimacy. Selfishness, which breeds "indifference," never allows one to care enough about the other to truly know him or her, whereas real love is able to meet needs physically and emotionally even without asking. Only God's design for a love affair does this.

The highest quality of earthly living is marriage as a love affair because it was God's design for mankind at the beginning. Proverbs 18:22 says, "Whoso findeth a wife findeth a good thing, and obtaineth favour of the LORD." A virtuous, Godly wife comes with a blessing. God's plan for earthly life is the best plan...marriage, between one man and one woman, living a love affair with those beautiful and strong emotions of infatuation under the umbrella of His love covenant. God designed husbands and wives, not children or unmarried adults, *especially* for earthly life. Children are simply in transit to becoming husbands and wives. Multitudes of unmarried adults only resulted when sin entered mankind; God said that it was not good for man to be alone (Gen 2:18), thereby creating *marriage* in *His image: holy, sinless, and full of love.* Adam and Eve were created perfect, without sin. God intended for perfect husbands and wives to have perfect children, growing in transit *to becoming* perfect husbands and wives, all living under the love covenant. *Just imagine* had sin not entered mankind. Perfect husbands and wives would have had perfect children growing up to be perfect husbands and wives, with each couple having rule and accountability to the calling or gifts that God gave them. We were to rule or have dominion over our gifts and the earth, not each other. That is why Jesus is called the "King of kings." In mankind was where God wanted to set up His earthly kingdom. We, as husbands and wives without sin, were to *rule as kings* as God, Jesus, and the Holy Spirit do. That is what God meant by "Let us make man in our image, after our likeness and let them have dominion...in the image of God created He him; male and female created He them, and... [told them to] replenish the earth, and subdue it: and have dominion…" (Gen. 1:28) Marriage was created in the image of the Trinity; they *ruled*.

Living single, though it is not a sin, is not God's best. When God said that it was not good for man to be alone (Gen. 2:18), He meant it. Singles choosing to remain single must realize that the very thing that is a blessing in marriage, sex, is a *curse* outside of marriage. That is why Paul said that it is better to marry than to fornicate or burn with desire (I Cor. 7:2, 9). It is because of the weapons of mass destruction that singles do not want to marry (except for the few like Paul). And that is very understandable; sin creates pain and destruction. Nevertheless, God gave the solution for this; the answer is in Jesus Christ and His love. ***All authority belongs to Jesus***. The love union God created to be experienced in a love affair *cannot* be experienced outside marriage.

It should be noted too that before sin entered the world, marriage was <u>absolutely</u> *the most beautiful thing you could ever experience*. It was God. It was God's fullest! *Adam and Eve were sinless and embodied God's total love*. <u>There was no pain there, no selfishness</u>. When they broke this pure covenant with God and sin entered, God sent Jesus Christ to make available again everything that belonged to marriage in the purity of its covenant. All we have to do is trust Him and obey. *It is available to us, truly!* All He asks of us is to *trust Him*…

"God alone gives the best gifts. You can't improve upon Him."
Deborah L. Rivera

With so many people believing that marriage is supposed to be an arrangement, that marriage as a love affair is just fantasy, many couples choose to *live together unmarried* to enjoy companionship and lust, never surrendering their hearts to the Holy Spirit to change them by God's love. Society has labeled this "common law," but the Bible refers to this as sin. Marriage is "oneness"—a commitment; shacking up holds on to two-ness—"non-commitment." Some couples believe that living together, doing everything including sex, lets them know how compatible they are; if things work out well, they get married. This is not building on a foundation of truth in rhythm with God's holiness and love. Man cannot improve or change what God has ordained. God made marriage to last an entire lifetime…as a love affair.

"God's Word proves itself.
Most people die lonely and unfulfilled, no matter how much they achieve.
You can't get around God's marriage as the highest form of earthly living. Nor can you alter God's marriage lived out as a love affair without perverting it and bringing a curse upon yourself, your children, and your grandchildren.
One may not believe this now, but time is on God's side. Again, at the end of life, you won't have to believe it; *God's Word will prove true.*

Let God be true, let every man be a liar (Rom. 3:4)."
Louis L. Forté

The dating couple in a love affair would want the best for each other and not bring sin to themselves before God by fornicating or living together with fornication. Fornication is having sex before marriage. The Bible refers to this as sin. Because God's love affair couple are already walking in God's intended love for one another, they are not afraid of marriage at all, so they do not feel the need to live together, being sexually involved prior to marriage: *They are eagerly awaiting it...like a treat*. They are in *utmost* anticipation to fulfill God's earnest *gift* of eros, sex, completely fulfilling their love affair. With their needs already met in the confines of agape and phileo (and soon eros) love, there is nothing to lose, only to gain. God's love in them creates strong faith in their inner man to view the long term of marriage as a beautiful journey and not as a selfish short-lived risk.

Dating couples of an arrangement are mostly afraid of marriage because usually they are not getting their needs met even while they are dating. They are experiencing selfishness, self-will, self-righteousness, and pride, so they are extremely doubtful of the future. God's purpose for a love affair is not in their relationship; where there is a lack of love, there is fear. It says in I John 4:18, "Fear hath torment. He that feareth is not made perfect in love."

"With the lack of God's intended love in *pre-marital arrangements*, <u>fear</u> of losing their own selfish desires dictates their decisions to avoid marriage. They don't realize that a love affair is all about giving.
Agape gives. Love gives. God gives.
Love is not in them."
Louis L. Forté

Someone submitted to the Holy Spirit is giving his future mate what he needs even before marriage, so he is not afraid of the future. Love is in him. Perfect love casts out all fear (I John 4:18). This is why living together is futile and not of God. Its foundation is *not* based on love but on fear.

Premarital sex, fornication, is also of Satan. Premarital sex does not come from agape, phileo, or eros love *because God is agape, phileo, and eros. He created them holy.* God says not to fornicate, so premarital sex cannot come from these. *Premarital sex comes from the lust of the flesh.* Fornication destroys trust in a mate after the marriage because it shows that he or she does not die to the flesh in this area.

Not only does God call us to die to our flesh daily; He also requires participants embarking on love affair to walk in the fruit of the Spirit. *Patience* is one of these fruits. Premarital sex will wait till the commitment before God has been unified. In an arrangement, dying to flesh and walking in the fruits of the Spirit are not valued, so flesh thrives and patience goes out the window, as does the love affair. Self-will and lust reign. There are many other situations that lead us to sin. We must follow God's blueprint of holiness first, then love our future mate before anyone or anything. If not, sin will destroy us, as all sin leads to death.

In a budding love affair of an *engaged couple*, agape, or God's love, is the *foremost love in their hearts* and what they put first in their relationship. It is the love that never quits; it is protective, honest, loyal, strong, reliable, full of wisdom, respectful, and selflessly giving; it always meets the needs of the other mate before its own and those of others. And it is like Christ in that it causes each mate to die for each other daily. It is strong as death.

Next, engaged love affair couples focus on phileo love; this is friendship love. Premarital couples will love each other in spending time together, having fascination in learning the other's uniqueness and likes/dislikes, enjoying learning what each one *needs* to feel completely loved, and enjoying learning how to love to last a lifetime. The characteristics of oneness – to serve, to protect and to please each other, will be the motive that governs each future mate when planning for housing, job security, family, etc.

Lastly, eros love is God's final gift that binds a couple in a covenant with Him after marriage vows have been taken. Its intimacy burns with passion and desire. It is *a gift* that is pure and bonding. It completes and grows a love affair in the most beautiful way. Many fail to realize that eros love on its own is lust because it was never created to stand without agape and phileo present as its commanders. When eros is led by agape and phileo, *it is pure* and will deepen for a lifetime.

"Agape and phileo must *lead* eros Or eros will never be God's love."
Deborah L. Rivera

It must be noted again that any kind of sin in a relationship is Satan's way to deceive couples and infiltrate the marriage. This is where generational curses to the third and fourth generation can be formed, because sin gives Satan legal right to attach himself to the marriage. If you are an unmarried couple and in fornication or being tempted to fornicate, or if you are involving yourselves in other kinds of sins, now is the time to ask yourselves, "Why am I doing this?" You do not want the repercussions of your sins to be brought on your love affair, your children, and your grandchildren. Many cases of alcoholism, fornication, molestation, drug addictions, sexual affairs or adultery, abuse, and incest have been passed down through generations.

This is why God demands holiness individually and as a couple, whether dating or married. All sin gives birth to Satan having some place in that person's life or marriage. <u>Sin does not just harm the sinner; tragically, it affects all who are around them</u>. Sin in a relationship will ultimately destroy that relationship and the relationships of the next generations if not turned around by the Lord. This is why God hates sin; we should, too. Adultery, ungodly behavior, and pride should not be named among us. We are called to run the race, not as beating the air, but as one striving for a prize (I Cor. 9:24–27). Our motives need to be clear. <u>We know that we are but flesh, but we run the race to live as holy, not accepting our fallen nature</u>. In ourselves, we cannot do this. But with the power of the Holy Spirit, we do not *have* to sin; He can keep us. He says, "Be ye holy, as I am holy" (I Peter 1:16). This is a command. He will not tell us something we cannot do. He gives His Spirit to help us do this. He says, "Walk in the Spirit, and you *will not* fulfill the lust of the flesh" (Gal. 5:16). You cannot walk in the Spirit and the flesh at the same time. One will rule each action.

To All

"The Bible teaches that God is love. If love is not in what you do for your mate, God is not in it."
Louis L. Forté

Remember, all of life is one big rhythm. Remove God's intended love for a relationship and life becomes useless, unfulfilling, insecure, boring, perverse, depressed, lackluster, corrupt, etc. Some people simply give up and die physically, but many are dead men walking, dead internally or emotionally. In this physical life, there is a component you cannot live without or else you will be dead emotionally: God's love. In the spiritual life, there is also a component you cannot live without or else you will be dead spiritually: God. To be dead in either regard puts you out of God's rhythm for life or out of His love.

"We cannot change God's original plan without suffering some death. God is God, and He cannot change. When we violate His truths, *we make His truth our greatest enemy*, there is no enemy more powerful, more relentless than rejecting His truth."
Louis L. Forté

Romans 3:4 says, "Let God be true, but every man a liar…" It is evident that God is eternal and we are finite. God's ways are higher than our ways (Is. 55:9). On earth, man's days are numbered. Not one day transpires during which someone does not prove that we are finite by dying. One day, time will end it all, and all of us will die. Did you choose a love affair or an arrangement? Man, born of a woman, lives but a few days; then, he must return to the one who gave him life and give account of the things He gave him: his relationship with God, his marriage, and the rest of life, just in that order. We must give account of how we have spent this fleeting time on earth. This is why agape, His love, is so important. When appropriated correctly, it funnels down from God through our spiritual body, then to our physical body, then to our mates, then to our children and our ministry, then lastly to our external family, friends, and livelihood. God's plan covers all the bases in the proper order of His wisdom and understanding. He's awesome; nothing is out of order or left undone. Look at the order in the universe. He never does anything without order. His ways are truly amazing. They bring fullness and fulfillment in every area of life.

"**To love is to live.**
Live life **to the <u>fullest</u>, and <u>get ready for glory</u>**!"
Louis L. Forté

If you are in a relationship, whether dating, engaged to be married, or married, what kind of relationship do you have— God's love affair or your arrangement? **Change is just a choice away.**

Invitation to Accept Jesus Christ as Your Lord

Father, I confess that I am a sinner. I thank you for sending your Son, Jesus, to die on the cross for my sins.

You said in Romans 10:9–10 that if I believe in my heart and confess with my mouth that you sent Jesus to die for our sins and that you, God, raised him from the dead,

I will be saved.

Father, I now receive Jesus Christ as my Lord and Savior. Come into my heart. I surrender my life to you and will live for you the rest of my life.

John 3:16

"For God so loved the world that he gave his only begotten son, that whosoever believeth in him should not perish, but have everlasting life."

The Marriage Love Affair Vow

I will never let anybody or anything come between God, you, and me.

In all things, under the love of God, I will put you first in every situation.

I promise to value everything that you hold important under the banner of God's love.

I'll let nothing change how I feel about you

As I purpose in my heart

To love you in His rhythm of love.

I take the LOVE COVENANT as my vow:

To love the Lord and our Savior Jesus Christ *with all of my heart, soul, and mind; more than myself, anyone, or anything in the world*

and

to love you *more than myself, anyone, or anything the world may bring.*

I vow to be yours to do with as you please

under the banner of God's love

for the rest of my life.

Let's start a love affair…

REFERENCES

Bevere, John. 1995, 2006. *Breaking Intimidation.* Florida: Charisma House, A Strang Company. Used by permission.

Briggs, Charlie. Personal quote. Lancaster, CA 2010. Used by permission.

Munroe, Miles. Keynote Speech. Bob Harrision Conference. Hawaii, 2007. Used by permission.

Strong, James, S.T.D., LL.D. 1985. *The New Strong's Concordance of the Bible: Concise Edition.* Nashville, TN: Thomas Nelson, Inc.

About the Authors

Louis L Forté

Louis L. Forté was born in 1941 to parents Walter E. Forté and Hattie Mae Forté in New Boston, Texas. Louis was the seventh son of his ten siblings, seven brothers and three sisters. It was during his early years that his parents taught him the importance of how God's Word affects everything in life. This training stayed with him when he moved to Los Angeles, California, in July 1959 to start a new life. He was diligent and committed to fulfilling his dreams, determined in his heart never to "settle" or accept less than the best in his life.

Four years after moving to Los Angeles, his dreams came to fruition. He met and married Sarita Del Sims, his love for life. They both loved each other, country-living, and the Lord. They were known by others as inseparable, always together. Louis and Sarita would greet each other by saying, "Hi, Me." They loved each other very much and were famous for being made for each other. Within the next several years, they had four children and a farm. Living in Christ's example was important to Louis and Sarita, and as parents, they taught the Word of God to their children at an early age.

Louis and Sarita enjoyed helping others. Whether it was Louis' giving a timely word of wisdom, helping countless people, or Sarita's blessing others with hospitality and kindness and the many talents the Lord had given her, their pair was a perfect match. They were both musically talented and sang beautifully together, enjoying being a light to others.

It was important to Louis to teach his family humility, the ability to change when you are wrong. It was his common practice to tell his children, "If you see me doing something wrong to your mother, or wrong in itself, tell me. I'll change." This was his life.

Yet, even with their ingrained love for the Lord, he and Sarita made mistakes from selfishness or a lack of understanding, and in the early 1990s, they lost everything…almost including their marriage. At that time, as a businessman and a general contractor, Louis went bankrupt after experiencing abundant success. But instead of giving up, becoming bitter, and blaming others, Louis humbled himself and took the blame for his actions. He refused to faint and instead pressed on to restore their livelihood and their marriage. He went to the Word of God. Certain scriptures that he needed at that particular time began to jump off the pages at him, so he committed them to memory. Soon after, one day, as he went to quote them, they came out as songs. Then, he began to sing these scriptures that he needed to deal with life's challenging situations.

He began to read approximately three to five chapters of the Bible a day to keep the devil at bay. Learning to never allow the devil to speak to him, he spoke the Word to the devil. When the devil would try to come back and torment his mind about all of his past mistakes, he would further sing the scriptures to the devil. In the early beginnings of his quoting scriptures, one time, the devil reminded him of something foolish or wrong he had done, so he told the devil, "If I am not praising God when you come, you are going to be my cue to start praising Him."

Louis knew that God was true to His promises to heal and restore his life, so he would not settle. He kept his focus on what God said only. He sees the change of restoration every day and welcomes the hand of God in his life.

Deborah L. Rivera

Born to parents Louis L. Forté and Sarita Del Forté, Deborah Lavora Forté (now Rivera) was introduced to the Lord at a very early age from the instruction and life example of her parents. Being the eldest daughter, she witnessed the arrangement lifestyle that developed between her parents. Instead of being affected adversely, she grew close to the Lord and made Him first in her life. The Holy Spirit began to groom her at age 12 in the ways of God's love for relationships. Studying the Bible and maintaining an intercessory prayer life were her mainstays throughout her entire teen years. She learned of the reality of God's love, His amazing power, and His unlimited abilities. She loved *the heart of God* and wanted to be used as a servant to introduce people to His great love and win the lost to Christ. It was at the verge of entering college that a new series of challenges presented themselves. The compromise of self-leading instead of being led by God began to take over. Right before she decided to go down her own path, she heard the Lord say, "I'm not in this decision you are making," but with these challenges ever so present, she yielded to her decision, and for the next several years, she lived by trying to make God fit into her world.

One night she heard the Lord tell her that if she did not turn around, stop trying to make Him fit where He was not leading, she would lose everything He had placed inside of her. She knew what He was referring to: *His love for the nations.* This love... that begins with marriages in His beautiful love of oneness, <u>and how through this, His love flows through the home to build everyone in the family, the community and then the nations</u>. In this one second of hearing the Lord's voice, His mercy deeply cut into her heart. Broken and contrite, she immediately repented, denounced her error, and never turned back.

The Holy Spirit began to groom her again in His love of oneness, though more explicitly since 1999. She spent hours studying the Bible and in prayer, letting Him lead *only*. The Lord's great love, faithfulness, and accuracy never fail to amaze her day by day. God's message for her to give to people is, "God's love and grace can change the hardest situation to His most beautiful and fulfilling love—He is the *master* of the human heart and loves us so much."

Deborah is now married and seeks to let the Lord use her in bringing the love of God's heart to the nations.

She dedicates this book to the Lord, and to the love of her life, her husband. **"Dearest Lord... All glory goes to You, and Joe, I love you more than words could ever express."**

Contact LovingForté at:

info@lovingforte.com

www.ingramcontent.com/pod-product-compliance
Lightning Source LLC
Chambersburg PA
CBHW071230290326
41931CB00037B/2619